Compassionate Commitment

GROWING TOGETHER THROUGH AWARENESS, EMPATHY & KINDNESS

Compassionate Commitment

Growing together through awareness, empathy & kindness

James Farwell

The Mindful Word

Published by The Mindful Word
An Imprint of Engaged Living Books

Copyright © 2019 by James Farwell

ISBN 978-1-77380-215-2 (paperback) | ISBN 978-1-77380-216-9 (ebook)

All rights reserved. No part of this publication may be reproduced, stored in a retrieval system or transmitted in any form or by any means—electronic, mechanical, photocopy, recording or any other—except for brief quotations, without the prior permission of the publisher.

Cover design: Mindlasher
Cover art: Peratek
Author bio photo: Matthew Farwell

Printed in the United States of America

The Mindful Word
1120 Finch Ave. W.
Unit 701-928
Toronto, Ontario
M3J 3H7, Canada

Visit us at www.themindfulword.org

Contents

Foreword	vii
Acknowledgements	ix
Introduction	xi

PART ONE: THE BASICS OF WHAT A COMMITMENT RELATIONSHIP INVOLVES

1.	The Need to Tend to Our Relational Garden	1
2.	What We Bring with Us into Our Relationship	5
3.	Our Attraction to Our Partner	10
4.	Falling in Love and the Inevitable Season of Struggle	15
5.	Three Options Open Up After The Struggle Stage Takes Place	18

PART TWO: THE ART OF COMMUNICATING WITH OTHERS

6.	Using the Same Words and Speaking Different Languages	25
7.	Sending and Receiving Undistorted Messages	32
8.	Learning to Listen to One Another	36
9.	The Art of Practicing Compassionate Communication	38
10.	Clarifying the Specific Components of an "I Statement"	43
11.	Clarifying The Specific Components of "I Statements"	45
12.	Clarifying Further Components of the "I Statement"	47

PART THREE: REAL LIFE ISSUES THAT CONFRONT EVERY RELATIONSHIP

13.	The Importance of Not Taking Things Personally	50
14.	Understanding More About Stress in Our Life	55
15.	Exactly What Is Being Mindful All About?	60
16.	Seeing Anger for What It Is	65
17.	Sexual Sharing: The Many Faces of Intimacy	71
18.	The Adventures of Becoming a Parent	77
19.	Relating to Hormonal Changes That Are Out of Our Control	81
20.	Living With Illness	84
21.	Living With the End of Life and Death	87
22.	What Place Does Counseling Have in a Commitment Relationship?	92
23.	Some Final Thoughts About Compassionate Commitment	96

Foreword

The first time I met Jim we didn't actually meet. Jim was accompanying his wife to an art class where I worked. His quiet presence in the back of the room stopped me in my tracks. In retrospect, the sensation struck me as similar to the jarring moment when you hear the sound of a foghorn on a large ship in the dark of night and you just know you have to pay attention. In many instances since then, I have marveled at Jim's quiet wisdom as he applies a few and quietly spoken healing words to situations at hand. I wish I had known Jim during my stormy years in the wake of a marriage ravaged by the break of trust following the unfaithful and secret extramarital affairs. I wonder if I would have or could have responded differently had I read Jim's words then.

It's funny how time works. I too have been working on a communications book as part of my own social-emotional life skills work for the last two years, and now I am honoured to write a foreword for Jim, who worked with one of the primary communications experts of our time, Marshall Rosenberg, almost 50 years ago – when I was a teenager. Certainly, Jim is one such expert now. His advice on relationship is profound. He makes it all sound so simple, because it is that simple, but most of us are far from mindful about the bigger picture and our own presence. It is so much less about what they can give us than what we can give them. Of course, Jim doesn't just make such sweeping statements, but backs them up with reasoning, practical advice and case studies from his own experiences as a relationship counselor.

Everyone who is or wants to be in a relationship can benefit from this book. Jim addresses many phases of our lives through the couple-hood lens: roadblocks to avoid for expecting parents; the hormonal phases of a woman's life, those which few men understand; men's equivalent andropause, which word few women likely know exists; having a child; becoming ill; dying. His suggestion of weekly couple's business meetings could benefit just about anyone.

Jim's authenticity, quiet charisma and authority of his subject gaze through the lines and right at you, reminding you to be present and mindful. Through actively listening and sharing we learn to truly hear the other, to be empathetic, to walk it their shoes – an increasingly forgotten skill.

Here, in a time of great ignorance of the art of communication we are witnessing the breakdown of relationships and inabilities to build new ones. Jim's book has the extraordinary potential to bring us closer together and heal our wounded understanding of togetherness. As more of us recognize that it starts within and starts with ourselves, Jim's book may serve as the missing tool for couples and people everywhere to begin building peace at home.

Bente Mirow
Forest Knolls, California
March 2019
www.InnerWeather.com

Acknowledgements

This book would have never been written had it not been for Jon Kabat-Zinn's bringing together of Buddhist Psychology with western psychology and medicine. His creating of a Mindfulness Based Stress Reduction program through the University of Massachusetts Hospital has transformed my view of life. My first exposure to Mindfulness was through attending his 8-week course offering through the Kaiser's Behavioral Health Program in San Francisco.

From that beginning, I began reading Jon's writing, and the writings of Thich Nhat Hanh, Eckhard Tolle, Jack Kornfield, Tara Brach, Adyashanti, Bob Stahl, Steven Hayes and Shauna Shapiro among others. These individuals served to deepen and further lead me in the development of my Mindfulness Meditation Practice.

My experience with Marshall Rosenberg, and his approach to nonviolent communication has served as a foundational underpinning in my relating to how people effectively communicate with one another throughout this text and throughout my personal and professional life.

I am indebted to Sonia Gonzales, the coordinator of Kaiser's Behavior Health Program in South San Francisco, who hired me to teach courses in Couples Communication. Those classes and class participants had an enormous impact on my developing a practical approach to relating to interpersonal life issues.

Had it not been for Anne Marie Dana Zadek's mentioning my writing to a stranger in a Sausalito coffee house one morning, who happened to be a freelance editor for Mindfulness based publications, I would have never contacted Jane Olivier of The Mindful Word. Jane not only became my editor, who edited my articles for the Mindful Word, but also took on the task of editing this manuscript. Her support and gift for writing and editing allowed the intent of what I wanted to say to come to fruition.

After the book was edited, Jane sent a copy of the manuscript to Kiva Bottero. He was enthusiastic about the book and he embarked on publishing it. His enthusiasm, suggestions and support, have led to the birth of this text for others to experience. For me, sharing and working with such a publisher is truly a profound gift.

When Kiva suggested that someone write a Foreword for the book, I asked a long time Mindfulness soul sister, Bente Mirow if she would be willing to do me the honour of writing the Foreword. She felt honoured to have been asked and beautifully captured the intent and essence of Compassionate Commitment: Growing Together Through Awareness, Empathy and Kindness.

My wife, Anne, as my soulmate, has encouraged my looking inward for my sense of direction and affirmation in my writing. I am forever grateful for her love and partnership in our life's journey together. Without our sharing, there would be whole vistas and aspects of life that I would have never come to know.

Introduction

In Buddhist Psychology, the underlying cause of all suffering is ignorance. Ignorance is not being aware of what you don't know.

This lack of awareness certainly impacts our lives and relationships in negative, often hurtful ways. It is as if we don't know what we need to do to make things work between ourselves and someone else. It is much like not being aware of social customs and, as a result, doing things that are offensive to others, all the while, not realizing what we are doing is wrong.

For many, coming into a commitment relationship can be like getting onto a roller coaster. The only difference is that instead of the ride beginning slowly and building to a crescendo, somewhere in the middle or towards the end, the ride often begins fast and can, then, decelerate to a stop unexpectedly for reasons that are not clear to either party.

There are very real reasons for these unexpected slowdowns and stops in every relationship. In fact, they are to be expected. Sooner or later all couples experience periods of upset, confusion and even pain. Such times can also serve as opportunities to grow as individuals and as relational partners.

The problem is that these seasons of struggle usually come as a complete mystery to the participants and often feel like a form of betrayal, or a kind of annoying power struggle. The person who you came together with as your ally begins to feel more and more like an adversary. In fact, all couples go through the realization that the person I was attracted to isn't the person I thought they were. The truth is that our partner is *much more* than we thought they were. We truly begin to realize that our partner has needs, feelings, fears, talents, hopes, blind spots, physical issues, etc. that we didn't anticipate when we first met and began our journey through life, together.

If we had been forewarned about these changes in our relationship, it would not be as perplexing to us. We might not have personally reacted to as much of what is going on. We would be better able to go from one season of upset to the next as a matter of course. To be sure, we would need to engage in the work that a relationship requires of us, however, our difficulties might have been better seen in a perspective that is understandable. If we had been more well prepared for such times of confrontation, we would be better able to travel the roads ahead and would benefit from an improved our connection with that someone with whom we have chosen to share our life.

The focus of this book is to provide you with information that will allow you to move from being unaware of what you don't know, to knowing what you need to know to make a relationship between you and someone who is important to you, be all that it can be for the both of you.

This book is committed to assisting you and your partner, whether in a gay or straight, bi-sexual or transgender relationship, in understanding what goes on between couples, how to deal with issues that present themselves in the normal course of being together, and how to develop loving and helpful ways to deal with issues that will arise in the course of your life together.

One of the most profound gifts of a conscious relationship is to realize that our partner's needs are as important as our own and that, in a real sense, our partner's needs become our own.

This is the potential that we each have as we consciously relate to someone we love, and for whom we care. As we relate with awareness, empathy and loving-kindness and share our lives with a special someone else, we learn that whole vistas of life and human experience open before us in a way not possible for us to experience by ourselves.

Life is our real teacher. When we are ready to learn, we are presented with what it is that we need to address in life. It is my hope that this book will provide insight and have a healing impact on the lives of those who will find life bringing us together in this sharing.

My warmest regards and best wishes to you and your partner.

PART ONE

THE BASICS OF WHAT A COMMITMENT RELATIONSHIP INVOLVES

1

The Need to Tend to Our Relational Garden

The image of tending to a garden comes to mind when I think about what it takes to nurture a relationship. As with a garden, we till the soil, water and weed to create and maintain a healthy environment for all to grow and blossom. A commitment relationship requires its own version of tilling the soil, weeding and watering.

During the five years that I was privileged to teach Co5uples Communication, part of the *Behavioral Health Education Program* with Kaiser Family Foundation, one recurring issue that couples experienced was how, over time, the time they spent together became less and less. The stress of work, money issues, taking care of older family members, and caring for children all took its toll on the couple.

During my time with Kaiser, we spent two and a half years rewriting the course curriculum. In our *Participant Handbook*, there is a page where two circles are drawn, one on the left side of the page and the other on the right. The instructions are:

In the left side circle write the ways that you, as a couple, spent time together when you first got together. They listed outings, the time alone, the intimacy shared, the different activities and involvements.

In the right circle, elaborate on how you now spend time together. Instead of time alone, intimacy shared, various activities and involvements, there was work, keeping up schedules, various time and emotional demands that extended beyond the couple's partnership.

When the couple was asked to discuss the two circles with each other, it became clear that times had changed and, over time, the demands of life had served as a wedge that kept them apart from one another, preoccupied and fatigued. What was insidious about this was how subtle the process of distancing between partners had been. One, two, three years had passed and it took two circles on a page during a Couples Communication Class to realize how little tending of the garden was taking place, and how emotional time apart was impacting two people who truly cared for one another.

Four Ways to Tend to Our Relational Garden

Once we realized that the relationships in the room had become distanced and our ally seems to be more of an adversary, we suggested four activities that were ways to emotionally tend to their relational gardens.

The first is to begin using *"sticky notes"* as a way to acknowledge their partner on a daily basis. If two people had drifted apart by unconsciously not emotionally connecting with one another, then using little notes to say "Hi, I love you," or a smiling face or "thinking of you," provide an opportunity to let one another know that the other is thinking about them on a daily basis. These notes can be placed in a binder that their partner may open in some meeting at work, or they can be placed on the bathroom mirror, or in the refrigerator or on the horn of the car, the pillow, on a milk carton.

These notes will consciously do what you have unconsciously not done, pay attention to your special person. As dumb as it might sound, this "Sticky Note" exercise actually made people feel acknowledged and better about themselves and each other. Our basic need as human beings is to *connect* with one another.

The second way to reconnect with one another is to have a *"daily debriefing session,"* preferably during some lull in the evening before going to bed. It is simply a time to share with one another what is going on in your life. The idea is for Partner A to listen for 10 minutes to Partner B *without* saying a word. Then, Partner B will share and Partner A will listen.

The objective of this exercise is to be *present* with your partner and to *listen* to what is going on with them in their daily lives. The task is not to problem solve their concerns, or to make judgments, it is simply to be present and to listen. When two partners begin to drift apart, their sharing time becomes a casualty of the distancing process. A daily debriefing provides for a reconnecting with one another, a way to dial back into what your partner is experiencing in their daily life activities.

A third way to reconnect with one another is to perform *"caring behaviours"* for one another. What is a caring behaviour? It is "a considerate behavior that can be accomplished in a few minutes." If you know your partner likes a back rub before getting up in the morning, or likes to cuddle before going to sleep at night, or likes to have you pour a cup of coffee for them at breakfast, or pick up a piece of dark chocolate on the way home from work or the market, do something for them that says I am thinking of you and that I care for you.

Each time these caring behaviours are done, they reconnect you. In this way, you begin to bridge the gap that has been created between the two of you by not tending to your relational garden. The idea here is to simply do one thing daily to get into the practice of thinking about the other.

It is suggested to sit down together and share things that you would like the other to do. This is simply a way of hearing what it is that your partner finds enjoyable for you to do for them. No demands. And with each caring behaviour performed an expression of appreciation will seal the deal.

A fourth way to reconnect is to have a weekly *"Fun Night."* Countless times throughout our Couples Communication Course, this was the most difficult task to carry out. Why? Simply because it often meant getting away from children, finding child care and going some place outside the home. For some, the logistics of the practice were daunting. The practice needn't be elaborate. Here are some ideas:

- Dinner night out
- Having a cup of coffee out
- Going for a walk in the neighbourhood park or on the beach
- Going for a meal at a favourite take-out or local restaurant.
- Walking the dog
- Window shopping
- Watching a DVD at home with a big bowl of popcorn
- Playing a board game that you both enjoy

Some of our couples actually counted attending their Couples Communication Course as a Fun Night. The idea is to take time, weekly, to be together and to enjoy doing something with the person with whom you enjoy sharing time together.

Research has shown that couples who share together, doing enjoyable activities, feel an increased sense of closeness and affection towards one another.

The essential need for a couple is to be *present* with one another. We need to *listen* to each other without judgment or the need to fix something. We need to be open to hear the other's needs, feelings, and concerns, to treat our partner's need as being as important as our own. Essentially, we need to take time to water and weed the relational garden that we share with that special someone we feel love and care for.

2

What We Bring with Us into Our Relationship – A Mindfulness Based View of How We Create Our Own Reality

The more you know about how relationships work, the better prepared you are to understand what is happening within yourself and between you and your partner. This journey into understanding begins with how we make sense out of our experiences as we grow up and move through life.

A relationship of true commitment turns a searchlight onto all of our experiences and feelings about what relationship has meant to us in our life. Our present moment relationships are influenced, in many ways, by our past experiences with people and life events. We bring with us our experiences of how men and women relate with one another, what it means to be a couple, to be a family member, whether or not our feelings and their expression are acceptable and what trust is or isn't. We carry the joys and sufferings of our past relationships with us as we move towards someone to whom we feel a sense of attraction.

Our openness to having a connection with another person that might lead to a commitment is based on our need for connection and completion… with ourselves and with one another. This is an inherent aspect of who we are as human beings. Our need as individuals is to connect with who we really are inside, our inner essence, and not who our thoughts say we are.

As we travel through life, we attempt to make sense out of our experiences with other people. We do this by creating storylines and narratives in relation to what is taking place around us. In as much as this discernment process begins as we begin to develop our language skills in early childhood, often our storylines and conclusions about ourselves in relation to the world of people reflects our limited cognitive development and our limited understanding about feelings and relational issues.

The consequence of this process is that often we create a false narrative about ourselves in relation to our parents, our world of people and what is going on around us. As children, our me-oriented view of life that all little people experience, often offers up a negative view of ourselves that is flavoured with guilt, shame and a deep sense that "I am not good enough," or that "I should be different than I am."

It is truly mind-blowing for a parent to find out what conclusions our little people have quietly drawn from their various experiences of people and events in their lives.

The little 6-year-old girl who feels responsible for mommy and daddy arguing, assuming that their upset is because of her having done something wrong. The reality of the situation about mommy and daddy's raised voices was because daddy failed to deposit a cheque and the mortgage payment bounced. Imagine what it's like for a parent to find out that their precious child has arrived at such an inaccurate conclusion, has created a false, painful storyline and narrative that is, in truth, a lie about who they are?

For a child to live with the pain, shame and stress of feeling responsible for family upset is all too familiar a story. How many children feel responsible for their parents' divorce? How many children feel responsible for keeping the family on an even keel when one or both of the parents are prone to drink too much or are in some way dysfunctional?

These misperceptions can also result from our inner sense that we are ugly or stupid or feel shame because we have freckles or wear glasses or braces or have curly hair or are not good in sports or have difficulty with reading. Our suffering in life is because *"We believe in a thought that is at odds with what is, what was or what will be."*–Adyashanti

Our suffering is the result of these thoughts about ourselves in relation to others and our life experiences that leads to our misperceptions of ourselves in relation to who we really are. Our *reactive thinking* begins in childhood, and continues through our adolescence and into adult life. We pile one storyline on top of another throughout our life. This is how our inner critic emerges as a presence and force in our lives.

If our inner critic were allowed to remain unconscious and remain as the definitive statement about who we are, we can take these hurtful pronouncements from our inner critic to our grave.

Ask Yourself:

- When and how have you experienced your own inner critic?
- What kind of messages does it present you with throughout your daily activities and encounters with others?
- What kind of self-talk/inner conversations, do you have with yourself from moment to moment throughout the day?

It has been estimated that 85% of our time is spent in either rehashing the past or in rehearsing for the future. We are either reliving the upset or are preparing for it at some time in the future.

Jon Kabat-Zinn has written that we are not our reactive thoughts, we are the *witnessing awareness* that *observes* our reactive thoughts, our words, our feelings and our behaviours. Eckhart Tolle wrote: "We are awareness disguised as people."

In creating storylines we look at life based on what we have concluded about our experiences in relationships with others. We relate to a new experience based on our previous painful experience. This creates anxiety in our lives. Anxiety is often defined as *"anticipating that we are going to meet something we are afraid of in the future."*

The painful experience we have had with our parents or other authority figures, how we experienced our needs and feelings being regarded and disregarded, is what we anticipate we will re-experience in new encounters with other people. The pain we experienced in not having our emotional needs met will be what we anticipate our experience will be in relation to someone with whom we might find ourselves becoming close. In doing this we are looking at our lives from the past and are not experiencing the present moment. We also tend to mind-read others' behaviour and anticipate the worst.

And, finally, our reactive thoughts always have us doing—we are always incomplete, we feel the need to get somewhere, we are forever setting goals, our activities are a means to an end and not an end in themselves and we feel as though we are never 'good enough.'

The more we are able to see what we have been doing to make sense out of our life experiences, the conclusions that we have arrived at that have developed our sense of who we are through the voice of our inner critic, the better able we are to acknowledge and unplug from our reactive responses to life and be in the present moment. Rather than reliving our experiences from the past or anticipating that our experiences will be a repeat of what we have experienced in relation to others, we have the ability to experience life anew, with a new openness to what is before us, being alive in the present moment.

Our Need to Pause

This process of bringing awareness into the present moment takes some getting used to. Usually we simply react according to our story lines. So to stop this habit, as Tara Brach has written, we need to *PAUSE* and *check in with ourselves*, to periodically stop and ask ourselves "what is going on inside of me, *now*?" We need to ask ourselves "What am I thinking, what am I emotionally feeling? How does my body feel, how is my body reacting?"

As we begin to get used to this checking in with ourselves, it becomes more of a natural process, more a regular part of our daily life experience. People often report that the simple act of pausing and reflecting on what is going on within themselves and acknowledging what is taking place within them, causes them to relax and get unstuck from their negative inner conversations, or physical tension, or rushing around to do this or that.

A Time to Sit and Be with Ourselves

We can also take some time each day and allow ourselves to just sit and get in touch with our breathing. Our breath can serve as an anchor point to getting in touch with the present moment. When we do this, our reactive mind often goes wild. Our thoughts may go everywhere. This is often referred to as experiencing our "monkey mind."

Each time we catch ourselves being caught up with our "monkey mind" we can acknowledge what is happening and return to the present moment. As soon as we acknowledge that we are not in the present moment, we return to the present moment. As strange as that might sound, it is really that simple.

3

Our Attraction to Our Partner – Our Quest for Connection and Completion

Have you ever wondered of all the people you might have chosen, what was it that attracted you to the person who is your partner? At the beginning of our eight-week Couples Communication class, we would ask this question. We had answers that ran the gambit of reasons:

- "I liked their smile."
- "I like their gentleness."
- "I liked their ass."
- "I liked their honesty."
- "I liked their positive energy."
- "I liked that they listened to what I had to say."
- "In their presence, I wanted to be my best self."

Of all the possible partners these class participants could have chosen, there were very specific qualities and characteristics that were part of their selection process. And each professed their love for the other and said that they found one another attractive, sexy, and fun and comfortable to be with.

Their reason for being in the Communication Class was out of a concern that things had begun to misfire and they felt a need to do something about it, or they wanted to prevent a future sense of being alienated from one another. Some couples actually anticipated that they needed to develop communication skills to better cope with issues that they anticipated would or could arise in the future.

COMPASSIONATE COMMITMENT

So when we say that our attraction to our partner is our quest for connection with and completion of our selves, what do we mean? Remember, how we arrived at our sense of who we are? Who we are has been defined by our reactive thoughts in relation to our experience of others and in relation to our life experiences. How our *Inner Critic* constantly tells us we are not good enough, or we feel shame or guilt and have a sense that we should be some other way.

When it is time for us to move beyond the false pronouncements of our inner critic and get in touch with an authentic aspect or quality or characteristic within ourselves that we are ready to connect with, we intuitively find someone in the outer world who personifies or mirrors back to us those qualities that we need to connect with within ourselves.

This process allows us to be connected with *who we really are* inside. This urge to get in touch with who we really are comes from the healthy *essence* that lives within us. We are an *essence* that is *awareness* and *compassion* at our core. We are the *witnessing observer* of what we think and feel. We are the compassion and human-kindness that wants our suffering to end. Who we are inside wants to be our friend in dealing with what it is that causes us suffering.

Let's say, as children, we have had to protect ourselves from our expression of feelings because it wasn't safe for us to say how we felt or even to express our needs. When it is time, in terms of our inner emotional clock, to connect with that part of ourselves that feels comfortable with our needs and feelings, we will find ourselves drawn to someone who is able to openly express their feelings and is comfortable with others' expression of how they feel, or who we feel has the potential to comfortably be with their feeling world. The person with whom we find an attraction mirrors back to us those qualities that we are ready to connect with within ourselves.

When a person is drawn to another, there is a reciprocal sense of connection that is taking place. There is a gentle emotional reaching out that is felt by the two individuals, who are beginning to relate to one another. Some would refer to this as an opening to a sharing of compassion that is acknowledging and affirming to both parties. If this mutual response does not take place, the potential for a partnership does not get off of the ground.

Other Avenues of Attraction That Are Available for Us to Take

Our need to connect with some aspect within ourselves that another puts us in touch with, is one avenue of attraction that is open to us. There are other avenues that can have importance in our lives.

Our relationships with our parents have a strong impact on how we view the feminine and masculine in our lives

If a woman has had a positive experience with her father, she may find a man like her father to be drawn to in her adult relational life. If her relationship with her father was a distant and painful experience, she might be drawn to a man like her father and attempt, with her partner, to have the relationship that had eluded her with her father.

I once had a woman in my practice who was married to a man very much like her father, distant and non-communicative. She knew after the first six months that she did not want to have him as her husband. She began working with me six years into their marriage.

As we worked on how she experienced her marriage, her frustrated need to have a connection with her father began to emerge as an issue that she realized was keeping her with her husband. As she was able to acknowledge what was happening, she realized that what she wanted to have with her father was not going to be forthcoming. The difficulty was that if she left her husband, she would also be giving up any chance to have the relationship with her father that she never had. Once this became clear for her, she left her husband—really her father substitute—and moved on with her life.

Our parents and parental figures, often times, are not the mother and father figures that we needed them to be in our lives. When we are able to acknowledge that our parents *do the best that they can do with what they have to work with,* we free ourselves from the hope that they will be what we need them to be.

We can begin to see them as the real people that they are. We are able to depersonalize how they related to us, or what they said to us. That doesn't give them a free pass for being hurtful in words and deeds, it simply refocuses their behaviour as *their* limitation and not that there is something bad or shameful about us.

This same dynamic can take place with a man in relation to an empty mother experience. If the mother was distant, her son might find a woman to fulfil his unmet need for the mother he never had. Again, I once knew a man whose own mother's need was to be taken care of by her 'fatherly' husband. The mother's need for her father connection superseded her ability to attend to her young son. Her son grew up and was drawn to an earthy, mothering sort of woman.

Another avenue of attraction that a man or woman might take has to do with their having *suffered emotional and/or physical difficulties* in their lives

For those who have suffered through illness and emotional trauma during their formative years, it is often the case that the attraction to another person has to do with sensing another person's similar experience of hurt and suffering. Our capacity for empathy and compassion allows us to connect with others who are suffering, or have suffered in their lives, and to give to them what we know we would have liked to have been given, or were given in our own experience.

Two individuals can be drawn together as a result of *the attraction of opposites*

If someone who is extroverted, outward-focused in the world of people, they may well be drawn to someone who is introverted—inward focused. Or the more thinking-oriented person may be drawn to someone who is more feeling.

The same holds true for those who are more grounded in the senses, "rocks are hard and water is wet", as opposed to those who are more intuitive in their approach to life—those who consider the 'whys and wherefores', the possibilities and potentials of what might be. The opposite is also true. We will go into this more fully in the discussion around how we can use the same words and speech two different languages.

Then, we have the type of opposite attraction that goes on between the "sweet girl next door" and the "biker rebel with greasy hair." These two characterizations are purposely overstated. I observed this type of attraction during my high school years. "Sweet Sue" who was one of the most popular girls in our high school class, was attracted to "Robert the Rebel." The pairing jarred many of us.

She would climb onto his motorcycle and take off and leave many of us wondering what is going on? How did the rebellious maverick capture the heart of the sweet girl next door? The answer to this might be that the sweet girl next door wanted to taste the fruits of being rebellious, and the rebel wanted to connect with the part of him that was quiet and gentle.

Our attraction to someone else can be the result of any combination of the above basis for connecting with someone else.

What aspects of attraction seem to apply to your connecting with your partner?

The more we know about what we bring with us into a relationship—what the basis of our attraction is to our partner—the better prepared we are to make sense out of what is going on in our lives with the person with whom we have chosen to share our lives.

4

Falling in Love and the Inevitable Season of Struggle

The attraction stage of a relationship can be truly magical and can serve as an important bonding experience between the couple. When two people find themselves attracted to one another, their focus becomes centred on one another. There is a magical quality about being together. They long to be with the other. When apart, their phone calls and emails and tweets are a lifeline without which they would feel alone and empty. Often the two seem to know what the other is thinking without a word being spoken.

The couple's intimacy is intense and exciting and can feel transformative to both partners. This is the spell that was cast over the mythical Romeo and Juliet. While the intensity of the experience can be made the brunt of jokes, when Romeo thought that his Juliet had been taken from him in death, he felt he could no longer live. He took his own life. At such times of falling in love, kings give up thrones, people change jobs and relocate to be with their partner, and poems are written. Such is the seriousness of this transformative season of coming together with someone else who allows us to come together with ourselves.

In this season of 'Falling in Love,' our partner serves as a mirror that reflects back to us what we need to connect with within ourselves. In essence, we are seeing an aspect of ourselves that we need to connect with in the person of our partner. The intensity of this experience is enhanced by the release of certain hormones that cause pleasure such as norepinephrine and dopamine. There is also a hormone—oxytocin—that is associated with bonding, trust building and the establishment of empathy.

The combination of these dynamics and hormonal enhancements adds intensity to the experience that is a profoundly human and is, at its best, a beautiful experience of sharing between two individuals. The tenderness, caring, excitement of sharing in all ways, is a precious aspect of our human experience.

References are made about "love is blind," "beauty is in the eyes of the beholder," this is "just infatuation, everyone gets over it." Others attempting to minimize the reality of what each partner is experiencing, only intensifies the resolve of the couple to remain thus connected.

The Season of Struggle

The coming together of two people who feel as though they are one, is only able to last for a period of time. The difficulty is that the 'one' are really *two* different people. That one is able to see certain essential aspects of who they are in the other person can only last until the spell is broken. No one—no partner—can live as an image carrier for long before they begin to feel stifled. When one partner begins to become freed of the magical spell that they have been living in, birth is given to a season of struggle.

For the one who is still smitten, the reflection that served to connect the partner with important aspects of who they are is no longer available. It feels as though the partner's mirror that has served to put the other in touch with themselves, has stepped back and has turned sideways. For the one who feels that they are being left, it can feel like an aching emptiness, a pain that is unbearable.

The more that the still smitten partner tries to re-establish what used to be, the more the partner who has stepped back pushes back against being the image of what the other person has needed them to be. What seems like a power struggle can ensue. For the one who feels left, it becomes a life-and-death struggle to remain connected with the source of their connecting with themselves. For the other it is a struggle to remain their own person, apart from their partner.

Upset is *always* the result of broken agreements. Whether the agreement was spoken, signed or assumed, an agreement that is not kept causes upset. It is often the case that it is not until the agreement has been broken that its presence is realized. No couple who falls in love realizes what it is that is taking place between the individual and their partner. Only when the dynamics of what is going on are changed, only then will the upset be realized about what was assumed to be true.

What Lessons Are to Be Learned By This Process of Struggle?

The first lesson to be learned is that this is a normal process between two people. It is a dynamic that gives birth to both partners in different ways. During the spell of being captivated by the other, both are being put in touch with certain aspects within themselves that they are ready to connect with. In the state of captivation, they are not really seeing the other person, rather they are seeing themselves and the fulfilment of their need, in the other person. When they are excitingly making love with their partner, part of the intensity of their lovemaking is that they're really making love with an aspect of what they need to connect with within themselves.

When the spell is broken, and one of the partners begins to distance themselves from the other because they cannot forever remain as an image, the birthing of a real relationship begins to take place. The two who are one becomes the two who are engaged and involved with one another. This season of struggle marks the birth of a *real* relationship between two *real* individuals.

5

Three Options Open Up After The Struggle Stage Takes Place

One: Calling It Quits

The first option is to call the whole affair quits. The push and pull to have things remain the same for the one partner and for the need to change for the other partner can become a power struggle that becomes tiring, non-productive and potentially destructive for one or both partners.

If things become stalemated at this level, it would be better for the two to go their separate ways. It often takes time, sometimes a matter of years, to arrive at the reality that the limitations of the connection one has with their partner are what they are, and that the limitations are insurmountable.

The experience of falling in love was not in vain, however. Any time we are touched by someone else on a deep level, it has been a worthwhile experience. We have been able to connect with some part of ourselves that has been in need of connecting with for us to become aware of new aspects of our inner emotional world.

The key is to appreciate what has taken place, what it is that our experience has put us in touch with, and what we can learn from the experience. If we are able to do this, in time, with the necessary healing, we are the better for the whole experience.

Option Two: A Silent Arrangement to Co-Exist

The second option of the season of struggle that is presented to us is to learn to peacefully co-exist with the person we are with. This arrangement is a course that is often taken by two people.

The need for connection with someone, the need to avoid a sense of loneliness, the need to have an emotional anchor point around which to live becomes the goal. In this process, two people will often keep their deeper feelings to themselves in order to stave off upset. Again, the need to be emotionally connected with someone is the goal.

In this arrangement, the two partners will occupy their lives with activities that don't rock the boat. They become involved with their work and their interests. Having children is often an option. For the mothering figure, having children provides a role and activities than can be satisfying.

Interests and hobbies can become an important part of each person's life. Involvement in the work world, with hobbies, sports, or other interests often occupy such a couple's lives. Other people may take on significant roles within each partner's world. People will look to have their needs on various levels met outside of their primary relationship.

Very often resentment can be present between the partners. The resentment can occur on different levels. One might be that the potential that they felt in their 'in love' stage of being together, didn't work out as they would have hoped it would. Once they got beyond the 'seeing-themselves-and-their-need-fulfillment-in-the-other' part of the involvement, there can be a sense of feeling betrayed, hurt with the emergence of resentment. The hope for the kind of closeness and completion that was felt to be their potential has evaporated.

Another source of resentment has to do with their dependency on the other for their sense of emotional security. Again the overriding need is to not feel emotionally isolated and lonely. When people feel emotionally dependent, they feel vulnerable. This sense of emotional vulnerability can create the need to find ways to protect oneself should any upset take place between the partners. Each knows the vulnerabilities of the other and will, at times of feeling under siege, touch the known nerve ending of their partner.

This type of arrangement—be it unconscious or conscious—can last for years. There is an ongoing lack of fulfilment about the reality of what is going on or is not going on between the couple. It is not surprising to find such an arrangement will end in divorce after years and years of living together.

One of the reasons for the ending of such a long-standing involvement might have to do with the need for one of the partners to make a course change in their lives. For one partner who has served as the homemaker, it might be a matter of developing an interest in attending classes at a community college and preparing to go into business for themselves.

Such a change in course would necessitate a total change in the agreements that were either assumed or were consciously agreed to at some previous time with their partner. If the couple cannot navigate such changes in their living relationship, things can go from resentment to frustration and end up with a sense of futility. It is not surprising to see many long-term relationships ending due to such course changes in life.

Option Three: Creating a Compassionate Commitment

Leaving the involvement and settling to co-exist with someone are two common ways to relate to the falling out of love phase of two people's experience of one another. A third choice exists. This choice is to create a *conscious compassionate commitment* with someone else.

What Is a Conscious Compassionate Commitment?

Compassionate commitment begins with the fact that, regardless of our differences and our difficulties, the reality is that *I cannot imagine a life without you*. It is acknowledging that you are not the person I thought you were. In fact, it is the realization that you are much more than I realized you to be as a person. It is acknowledging that there are two people, two individuals in this partnership and not just a mirror that reflects aspects of what I need to get in touch with to connect with who I am, inside. It is the beginning of the establishment of a real relationship between two real people.

In order for this to be possible, there has to be an affectionate bond that exists between the two people. That was something that was absent with the couple who elected to go their separate ways. Instead of two people electing to co-exist, we have two people who are willing to take responsibility for relating to their own feelings, needs and suffering and to respect and support their partner in their relating to their feelings, needs and suffering. It is a commitment that says that your needs are as important as mine, and that, in fact, your needs ultimately become my needs.

This compassionate commitment relationship focuses on both partners doing what facilitates their own and one another's growth and, in so doing, supports the growth of the relationship. Does this sound like some kind of idealistic pie in the sky notion, or is it real, is it possible?

There are no losers in this sharing. There is only being fully present, cleaning up the unconsciously carried baggage that each partner has, so that past experiences of the two individuals do not interfere with what is happening in the present moment of what is going on between them, moment by moment.

The following is a poem that speaks to the nature of compassionate commitment:

The Gift of Love

To love someone for themselves
and not as an extension of who I am
or, what I need them to be…

To view someone else's needs as being as important
as my own…

To cherish my partner's being
as a gift to be acknowledged,
and nurtured…

Moving beyond myself,
into another's universe…

The union of opposites
and shared values…

To be a whole person
yet, interdependent…

Merging together, transcending
our singular gifts…

Experiencing a oneness that requires
commitment to achieve…

The gift of love,
the utter joy of such a partnership…

Experiencing the deepening essence of life
that only such a journey provides…

COMPASSIONATE COMMITMENT

The manifestation of the Divine's living
and healing Essence, within,
and between each one of us…

Thankful am I, for the gift of love.

PART TWO
───────────

THE ART OF COMMUNICATING WITH OTHERS

6

Using the Same Words and Speaking Different Languages

Everyone experiences and interprets the world differently. Two people can experience the same event and have two diametrically opposite experiences of that event. The reality of their different experiences needs to be appreciated as being equally valid. In truth, they *are* equally valid. The difficulty arises when one person judges the other's experience as being "wrong." When this happens, any effort at communicating with one another shuts down. Such judgments only promote defensiveness between two individuals.

Two Basically Different Ways of Approaching the World and People

There are two different types of interacting with the world in which we live. One is to look *outside* of ourselves. The other is to look *within* ourselves. According to Carl Jung, the noted Swiss psychiatrist, individuals are either *extroverts* or *introverts* in their approach to living their lives.

What Does It Mean to be an Extrovert?

These people are drawn *outside of themselves* for involvement. The energy of what is taking place outside of them engages and stimulates their interests and the nature of their involvement with people and life experiences.

Extroverted people like relating to other people. They enjoy parties and activities that engage them with others. When they are around a partner who is ill, their inclination would be to make chicken soup and engage with their partner in making certain that everything is all right. They will make certain that their loved one has taken their medication, that they are comfortable and that all of their needs have been met. Incidentally, this is the way that they would like someone to relate to them when they are not feeling well.

What Does It Mean to be an Introvert?

Introverted individuals are the polar opposite of the extrovert. They find themselves looking *within themselves* rather than outside of themselves to experience a sense of connection with what matters to them. Instead of responding to outside activities, they find themselves grounded by their own inner energy.

They recharge by having "down" time and being left alone. Rather than attending parties, they would prefer to read a book or take a solitary walk on the beach. If they were to go to a party, they would either sit by themselves, or if they found someone that they resonated with, spend the time being with that person and not randomly mingling with a group of people.

When an introverted person becomes ill, they want to be left alone. They want to be able to sleep, recover or die without being disturbed. The extrovert will offer chicken soup and back rubs while the introvert will recoil from their attention and feel overwhelmed and feel irritated by the behaviour of their partner.

The consequences of these two different approaches, if left as unconscious reaction patterns, are that the extrovert will feel hurt as they interpret the introvert's request to be left alone as a form of rejection. The introvert will feel their partner is insensitive and disregarding of their needs to be left alone and will become annoyed. Do you find this type of difference in your relationship with your partner?

Differences in Our Way of Relating to the Daily Realities of Living Life

Carl Jung suggests that there are basically four different ways that people *function* and relate to their worlds of people, activities and needs. According to Jung there is—the *Thinking Type*, the *Feeling Type*, the *Sensation Type* and the *Intuitive Type*.

To refer to us as a "type" is a way of saying that we all have our best ways of dealing with daily life issues. Some of us are more thinking oriented, others are more feeling oriented. That doesn't mean that a thinking-oriented person doesn't have feelings. Some of us are more able to deal with the givens of what we see or what is being said. Then, there are those who look at the possibilities and potentials of a situation.

We are all able to think, feel and relate to things through our senses and are able to relate to the possibilities and potentials of something. For most of us, one of these ways of dealing with the day-to-day reality is dominant, one is recessive, lying buried deeply within us, and the other two are sort of available, if we try to access them when relating to some issue that needs to be addressed. Ideally, when we need to relate to something through thoughts or feelings or through senses or through relating to the possibilities and potentials of a situation, we will have these abilities available to us.

The Thinking-oriented Person

This person relates to the world through ideas and concepts. Thinking-oriented people relate to their world through words and can take both sides of an argument with equal ease. They relate to life in terms of what is "logical" and are not necessarily emotionally involved in the position they have taken.

The Feeling-oriented Person

This person relates to people and situations based on how they feel about people and situations. Something is good or bad, right or wrong. Feeling types may not be able to put what they feel into words at a given time, but they "just have a gut feeling" about something, or someone which is the basis for their response.

Thinking and feeling people are polar opposites, and they are often attracted to one another. When these two get together they may be hearing the same words but speaking two different languages. The world of ideas and concepts collides with the world of right and wrong, good and bad.

For the thinking person, the feeling partner makes little sense since there are often no facts to back up their decisions and for the feeling person, the thinker is all in their head and is experienced as insensitive.

When these two opposites types get into an argument, the thinking person is usually "the winner." They can take what the feeler says and use it to undermine what the other person is attempting to say. For the feeling person, they know what they feel but often have a difficult time putting what they feel into words.

Often, after a verbal encounter, the feeling person will finally connect with what it is that they wanted to say, sometimes around two in the morning, and will want to wake up and engage their partner in another round of verbal sparring.

The Sensation-oriented Person

The sensation-oriented person engages people and situations by using their five senses: hearing, taste, touch, smell and sight. For sensing types, if they can sense it, it is so. For these people, "rocks are hard and waters wet." These people are able to make decisions based on the "isness" of what the senses tell them is true. If a partner tells a sensation-type person that they love them, the sensation-oriented person will believe that is how they feel. Why? Because their partner has said so.

The Intuitive-oriented Person

Intuitive people relate to the world in terms of possibilities and potentials and in the "whys and wherefores" of what they find before them. From a few facts, these individuals can quickly see the big picture without obsessing about all the details required to get from Point A to Point B.

Intuitive people can either be spot-on or off the mark by miles. I am an intuitive and, while at a party given by a woman friend, I was scanning the room and getting an overview of where people were in their interactions with one another. I saw a man and a woman interacting and made the mental note that they had something "going on" between them.

The next time I saw my woman friend who had given the party she looked like a truck had run over her. I asked her what was going on to make her look unhappy and distraught? She indicated that she and her husband had separated. We talked for a while about what had led to their decision to separate. She indicated that he had left her for another woman. I asked was it the blonde woman who her husband had been interacting with at the party? She looked at me and said yes, how did I know? Sadly, this time my intuition was spot-on. Such is the way of the intuitive.

Sensation and Intuitive people are also polar opposites and they, too, tend to attract each other. When a sensation-oriented person gets together with an intuitively oriented person, they find themselves using the same words but are speaking two different languages. The sensation person will look at the specifics of what their partner is saying and base their decisions on this, while the intuitive will not want to bother with specifics but, instead, will focus on the big picture and the end result.

When it's the intuitively oriented person who is in charge of balancing the chequebook, they will be content with "this is the more or less of our balance," while the sensation-oriented person will want their account balanced to the penny.

How Do You Think This May Impact Communication Between Two Partners?

Often, when individuals with these opposite ways of approaching life are attracted to one another, they require assistance in having what they are saying to one another translated by someone else so that they are able to understand what it is the other is saying to them.

In one of our Kaiser classes, there was a couple who had been together for over fifty years. While they felt love for one another, much of their shared life had not been all that enjoyable. They had recently returned to living together, after a trial separation that lasted less than six weeks. They found that life apart was even more disturbing to them than the frustrations of their daily existence living together.

When we began our class on "How We Can Use the Same Words and Be Speaking Different Languages," after the presentation on how people approach life from their different ways of seeing reality, they both shared their realization that *this was their problem*. They lamented that "if they had only known this years before…"

It is a premise of Buddhist psychology that *ignorance is our primary cause for suffering*. In all relational matters between individuals, if we are able to climb into the world of the other person, we will be able to begin to understand where they are coming from and what their experience is about. We will better be able to express empathy and compassion towards their frustrations and be able to acknowledge their perspective of reality, along with their needs and frustrations.

COMPASSIONATE COMMITMENT

The other thing about this process of being with your opposite is that, over time, each person can come to develop that part of themselves that is in need of developing. In essence, we can learn from one another. The intuitive can become more comfortable with relating to life through their senses and the feeling person can become more comfortable with relating to life through their ideas and thoughts and the thinking person can become connected with their feeling world.

This arrangement of forces is, in part, one of the basis of the old notion that opposites attract. This is not to say that it is impossible for two people who are similar in their ways of dealing with life to come together. When two such similarly oriented individuals become partners, they will usually be spared the frustration of using the same words and speaking different languages. In their case, they are coming to life from the same perspective and will have fewer misunderstandings based on their viewing life from a foreign life perspective.

7

Sending and Receiving Undistorted Messages

So often it's our ignorance that interferes with our ability to send undistorted messages to our partner. Our selection of words, our thinking that we are expressing our feelings when, in fact, we are expressing an interpretation or judgment of something interferes with our ability to communicate with another person.

Both judgments and interpretations are guaranteed turnoffs when attempting to communicate with someone else because they often elicit from our partner a perceived need to defend themselves. Open communication is not possible when one or both partners feel that they have to defend and protect themselves.

There are several foundation-laying thoughts that are essential to starting off on the right foot when attempting to communicate with someone else, especially your partner:

- To begin with, both partners need to be committed to opening up and sharing with one another.
- Each person's experience needs to be seen as valid. Each partner may have totally different experiences of the same situation. However, both partners' experience must be treated as being *equally valid*. Otherwise we are setting up a situation where one person is right and the other person is wrong and we promote the need to defend our self against the other. This need to protect ourselves when communicating with our partner is counter-productive.
- It also needs to be understood that words are powerful. People who were supposed to love and care for us have

sometimes expressed words that have been the cause of pain for us. We have, over time, learned to protect ourselves from such hurt, so we have developed ways to distance ourselves from others in conversation. How many of us, instead of actually listening to what someone else is saying, find ourselves formulating our response in relation to what someone is saying to us, while they are speaking? Some refer to this as a "yes, but" way of protecting ourselves from others, and we do this sort of thing quite unconsciously.

Over time, we develop and find ways to defend ourselves from being uncomfortable in conversations with others. We often develop listening blocks that not only distance ourselves from others, they also totally destroy our ability to truly share with someone else.

Here is a list of common listening blocks that are commonly used to protect us from being hurt by what others might say:

Ordering, directing and commanding—Telling the person you are conversing with to do something, giving orders and or commands.

Warning, threatening—Telling the person you are having a conversation with what negative consequences will follow if they do something.

Giving advice, solutions—Telling the other party how to solve his or her problems.

Arguing, lecturing—Trying to influence the other party with facts, counter-arguments, logic or your own opinions.

Judging, criticizing, blaming—Making negative judgments or evaluations.

Praising, placating–Offering positive judgments that may be interpreted as manipulation or attempts to influence the other person.

Name-calling, ridiculing, shaming, being sarcastic–Labeling or hinting that the party is foolish, unworthy of respect, shameful.

Mind reading, interpreting, analyzing–Telling the other party his or her feelings, thoughts or motives, or analyzing what he or she is doing or saying. Communicating that you have the other person figured out.

Sympathizing, reassuring–Trying to make your conversation mate feel better by talking him or her out of his or her feelings, or denying the feelings.

Interrogating, questioning–Asking continuous questions to try to find reasons or causes. Taking over the conversation for your purposes and not those of your conversation mate.

Interrupting–Finishing the other party's thoughts or constantly intruding with your comments.

Sidestepping, distracting, humouring–Trying to get your conversation mate away from the problem. Kidding her or him out of her or his feelings, pushing the problem aside or changing the subject—withdrawing from the problem.

Half-listening or paying partial attention–Pretending to listen while doing other things like chores, paperwork, watching TV, using body language that shows you're distracted, closed off or not listening.

Withdrawing–Shutting off the conversation, verbally or physically leaving without the other party's agreement or without any agreed to plan to resume the conversation at a set time.

Whenever we use listening blocks, we block our ability to be present and open with the person with whom we are attempting to

COMPASSIONATE COMMITMENT

communicate. This is counterproductive and is so often something that we are unconsciously doing.

Again, so much of what interferes with our ability to communicate with someone else is our lack of awareness of what we are doing to sabotage our attempts to talk with and share what we have to say with our partner. The next chapter will provide us with an understanding of how to actively listen to what our partner is saying to us.

8

Learning to Listen to One Another

How can we tell if someone is really listening to us? In our Couples Communication Classes we used a sharing and listening exercise that really gets to the heart of how much we are actually paying attention to what our partner is saying to us. It's helpful to actually experience the process of going through something like this to mindfully, consciously and with awareness, experience the process of actually *listening* to your partner. You might give it a try and see for yourself what happens.

Couples Exercise in Sharing and Listening

In this exercise, choose which partner will be the *sharing partner* (the one that is speaking), then, the other partner will be the *listening partner* (the one that is listening).

- The sharing partner will have the opportunity to tell the listening partner about the most frustrating thing that happened to him or her, today or within the past week.
- The listening partner will then restate what he or she hears the sharing partner saying to them.
- The sharing partner will then be asked if what the listening partner states was an accurate expression of what was said.
- If not, the sharing partner will restate what he or she wanted to share with the listening partner.
- A second debriefing will take place.

Or, if the listening partner stated accurately what the sharing partner had said, then the roles are reversed and the sharing partner becomes the listening partner and the previous listening partner will become the sharing partner.

Typically, it doesn't take more than two tries for each partner to accurately restate, to paraphrase what their partner has said to them. Often the partners heard what each is sharing the first time. The helpful part of this exercise is to be able to experience how we, each, routinely interact with someone who is attempting to communicate with us.

What we have just engaged in is an example of what is often termed "active listening." In the process of active listening we use paraphrasing what our partner has said to us as a means of communicating that we get what the other person has shared with us.

There are two other components to successful active listening. Along with our accurately restating back to our partner what they have said to us, the next step in active listening is *validation*. Validation means that each partner affirms the internal logic of the other partner's world. In other words, *one can stand in the others shoes and see how things appear to them*. In this, we need to suspend our view of the world and enter the world of our partner.

The third aspect of active listening is *empathy*. Empathy is the action of being aware of, being sensitive to the feelings, thoughts and experience of the other person. A statement like "how does this make you feel?" or, "can you share with me what you are feeling?" can assist in our being able to truly connect with what our partner is attempting to share with us.

9

The Art of Practicing Compassionate Communication

So, now that we have a sense of what it is like to consciously send and receive messages with our partner, we need to explore other potential blind spots in our perception of the actual mechanics of communicating with another person.

As was previously stated, it is our ignorance in understanding the differences between what is an expression of feeling and an expression of judgment or interpretation. An expression of feeling framed in an I Statement will *never* create the need for someone else to feel that they have to protect themselves when talking with us.

An expression of judgment or the use of any of the listening blocks we discussed previously *will* create the need on the part of the listener to defend themselves or to turn them off from being open to further sharing with you.

Marshall Rosenberg was my, and a great many others, mentor in the field of communication. He developed the Nonviolent Communication approach to people conversing with one another.

Rosenberg devoted his life to facilitating communication between people with the belief that with the use of nonviolent communication skills, peace is possible between couples, within families, within communities and in relationships between countries of the world.

I met with a group of San Francisco Unified School district staff and Dr. Rosenberg in the early 1970s to develop our school staff's ability to better communicate with one another. We would meet monthly to have sessions with Rosenberg, to learn about his views of communication and to develop the skills that would make it possible for us to utilize his approach to communication between ourselves as staff, and with our children in our various roles within the district.

Marshall Rosenberg spent a year meeting with staff, sharing with us how to communicate with one another in a respectful, compassionate way. Our Kaiser Couples Communication program integrated his approach into working with couples.

The following sections of this chapter and Chapters 10, 11 and 12 is, in part, material from Marshall Rosenberg's *Nonviolent Communication, A Language of Life, Second Edition*.

Marshall Rosenberg has given his permission to use his material in an effort to facilitate communication between individuals and groups. His only stipulation is that he is given due credit for what is being presented.

The Use of "I Statements"

(We are using a three step condensed version of Rosenberg's communication format instead of his four step approach. We are omitting a Statement of Need. Our intent is to focus our attention on statements of Observation, Feelings and Requests)

Statement of Observation and Fact–When _____
(just the facts)

Statement of Feelings–I feel _____
(express feeling)

Statement of Request–I wish/want/would like _____ (request).

In the Observational Statement, state *Just the Facts*:

- "When you get home two hours later that you said you would."
- "When you drive 70 miles per hour on a mountain road."
- "When you walk away when I am talking with you."

In the "I feel" statement, state the feeling in one or two words—use the Feeling Chart to assist you:

- "When you get home two hours later that you said, *I feel anxious, or I feel worried.*"
- "When you drive 70 miles per hour on a mountain road, *I feel afraid.*"
- "When you walk away when I am talking with you, *I feel hurt or angry.*"

In the request statement, state your *POSITIVE* solution in terms of a specific *behavioural* change:

24. For the statement: "When you get home two hours later than you said, I feel anxious. *I would like you to call me when you know you'll be late.*"
25. In the second example: "When you drive 70 miles per hour on a mountain road, I feel afraid. *I would like you to drive no faster than the speed limit,*"
26. In the third example: "When you walk away when I am talking with you, I feel hurt. I would like you *to stay with me until we conclude our conversation.*"
    - ✓ Deal with one area at a time
    - ✓ Be specific
    - ✓ Ask for a *behavioural* change (not a personality change)
    - ✓ Ask partner for his/her ideas and suggestions

This is an easy framework to incorporate into your approach to communicating with someone else. "**When** you do this or say that... **I feel**... **I wish, want or would like...**" In time, with practice, this orientation will become second nature to you. And, it is guaranteed to not pour fuel onto the beginning of a fire of upset between two people.

Remember we said that ignorance is at the root of our suffering? If we are ignorant about what a feeling is, we will unknowingly start on the wrong foot. It's frustrating to want to do the right thing to make our ability to communicate with someone work, only to find that we have made a judgment when we thought that we were making a statement of feeling.

To clear up this type of confusion, you will find lists of feeling words to help you become familiar with what words actually express feelings. Go over this list of feeling words and identify those feeling words that would be YOU to express in conversation with someone else.

Feeling Words When My Needs Are Being Met

Words of happiness: "I feel _____"

Excited	Cheerful	Contented
Touched	Joyful	Relieved
Pleased	Complete	Comfortable
Lucky	Lighthearted	Delighted
Restored	Optimistic	Satisfied
Hopeful		

Feelings We Are Likely to Feel When Our Needs ARE NOT Being Met

Words of unhappiness: "I feel _____"

Sad	Lost	Exhausted
Bitter	Hurt	Disappointed
Bored	Lonely	Pessimistic
Guilty	Regretful	Burdened

Wounded	Helpless	Miserable
Tired	Negative	Discouraged
Tearful	Worn out	Depressed
Hopeless	Heavy	
Crushed		

Words of anger: "I feel _____"

Angry	Annoyed	Vengeful
Exasperated	Inpatient	Irritable
Insulted	Frustrated	Mad
Aggressive	Enraged	Disgusted

Words of anxiety: "I feel _____"

Cautious	Worried	Afraid
Hesitant	Embarrassed	Distrustful
Self-conscious	Suspicious	Rushed
Anxious	Caught	Threatened

Other assorted feelings: "I feel_____"

Confident	Curious	Envious
Interested	Apologetic	Determined
Mischievous	Puzzled	Skeptical
Mystified	Obstinate	Confused

Again, select from these lists, those words that *you* would use to express how *you* feel and get used to thinking in terms of using these words in expressing how you feel with your partner.

10

Clarifying the Specific Components of an "I Statement"

Separating an Observation from an Evaluation

In the "I Statement," the first part has to do with *when* something happens. Often this statement is not entirely clear. This can be due to confusion between making an *observation*, which is a part of the 'I Statement' and an *evaluation or interpretation* of what has happened that is not a part of the 'I Statement.'

1. In the statement "John was angry with me yesterday for no reason" is this an evaluation of what is true, or an interpretation of what is true? This would be an example of an interpretation of John's behaviour. It's assumed that John is angry and that there was no reason for his assumed anger.
2. How is this statement different from the statement in the first example? "Yesterday evening Nancy bit her fingernails while watching TV." This is an observation. Nancy's biting of her fingernails while she was watching TV was an observable fact.
3. "Sam didn't ask for my opinion during the meet." Is this an observation or an evaluation or interpretation? It is an observation. Sam did not, in fact, ask for my opinion during the meeting.
4. "My father is a good man." This would be an evaluation on the part of the father's child. Beyond the child's experience, we don't know how the father behaves with others.

5. "Janice works too hard." Is this a statement of fact, evaluation or interpretation? It is an evaluation. A statement of fact would be, "Janice puts in 12 hours of work at her desk daily, and works, again at her desk on Saturdays and Sundays from 12 to 5."
6. "Henry is aggressive." Someone being aggressive depends on what being aggressive means to the person who is doing the observing. This is an evaluation.
7. "Pam was first in line every day this week." Was this an observable fact or an evaluation? It is an observation. It is a statement of fact.
8. "My son often doesn't brush his teeth." How is this example different from the example in the previous example? "Often doesn't" is not a specific fact, rather, it is an interpretation.
9. "Luke told me I didn't look good in yellow." That he *made* the statement is a fact and is an observation.
10. "My aunt always complains when I talk with her." Is this an observation, an evaluation or an interpretation? This is an evaluation of what the aunt does when she talks to her niece or nephew.

11

Clarifying The Specific Components of "I Statements"

Are We Expressing Feelings or an Opinion?

In our Couples Communication Course it became clear, early on, that the assumption that people know what a feeling is, is not true. The confusion between a *feeling* and an *opinion* is seemingly ingrained within us in our communication with others. This confusion wreaks havoc on our attempts to say what we want to say and to be heard by our partner and others.

It has been in relation with those to whom we are close that things have been said that have been hurtful for us. Our need to protect ourselves quickly mobilizes our defences at times when we feel incorrectly evaluated or interpreted or defined by someone's opinion of us.

In the following sentences, pick which of these sentences expresses a feeling and why. Then, reflect on the commentary that has been provided.

1. "I feel that you don't love me." Whenever we find ourselves saying "I feel that" we are in all probability going to express an opinion. This *is* an opinion and not an expression of feeling.
2. "I'm sad that you're leaving." When we make a direct statement and express a feeling, it leaves little to the imagination about what is being said. This is an expression of a feeling.
3. "I feel scared when you say that." Again, this is a pretty direct expression of a feeling. It leaves little to the

imagination about what is being said.

4. "When you don't greet me, I feel neglected." This is not a feeling. It is an interpretation of what the speaker thinks the other person is doing to him or her.
5. "I feel happy that you can come." Compare this statement with "I don't feel that you love me," or "I feel neglected." The "I feel happy leaves nothing to the imagination about what the speaker is communicating, the others are more nebulous.
6. "You're disgusting." Does that sound like a feeling or does it sound like an opinion? It's a statement of an opinion.
7. "I feel like hitting you." If you were to say, I am angry with you, and I feel like hitting you in the face, that would be an expression of a feeling. "I feel like hitting you" expresses what the speaker imagines doing, rather than how the speaker is feeling.
8. "I feel misunderstood." This is more of an expression of what the speaker thinks the other person is doing. A statement of feeling would be "I feel frustrated." Again, the difference between a feeling and an opinion is the specificity of what a person is saying about how they feel.
9. "I feel good about what you did for me." Though the word "good" is vague, it is a feeling. Other feeling words would include relieved, encouraged and gratified.
10. "I'm worthless." This is more of an opinion about how the speaker sees himself than an expression of a feeling.

12

Clarifying Further Components of the "I Statement"

Are We Requesting a Behavioural Change, Or Not?

So far we have discussed our observation about something happening whether it was an observation or an interpretation or an evaluation. We discussed the need to specify the facts of the matter.

We also discussed whether we are clearly expressing our feelings or are we, instead, expressing an opinion.

Now we are going to explore the third aspect of an 'I Statement,' the making of a request for a behavioural change in the person with whom we are interacting.

In the following list of statements, pick which of these sentences express clear requests for a specific behaviour change in the person with whom we are interacting.

1. "I want you to understand me." Is this a clear message requesting a specific behavioural change? No, it is a non-specific request that is unclear about what is wanted on the part of the speaker. A request for a specific action might be: "I want you to tell me what you heard me say."
2. "I'd like you to tell me one thing that I did that you appreciated." This is an example of a specific behavioural request being made in relation to the person with whom the speaker is interacting.
3. "I'd like you to feel more confidence in yourself."

This is too vague a statement that is requesting what, specifically, of the person? A suggested alternative statement would be "I'd like you to take a course in assertiveness training, which I believe would increase your self-confidence."

4. "I want you to stop drinking." What does the speaker really want of their partner? Their request is asking for what they do not want, rather than a specific request for a specific action. A more direct request would be "I want you to tell me what needs of yours are met by drinking, and to discuss with me other ways of meeting your needs."
5. "I'd like you to let me be me." Is this a specific request for a behavioural change? A more specific behavioural request would be "I'd like you to tell me if you become angry when I share with you how I feel about something."
6. "I would like you to be honest with me about yesterday's meeting." What is this request asking specifically? A more specific request would be "I'd like you to tell me if you agreed with how I structured the meeting."
7. "I would like you to drive at or below the speed limit." This is an example of a specific request for a behaviour on the part of someone else.
8. "I'd like to get to know you better." What specifically is the speaker asking of the person with whom the speaker is talking? A more specific request would be "I'd like you to tell me if you would be willing to meet for lunch once a week."
9. "I would like you to show respect for my privacy." What is this request asking for? A more direct request would be "When I am in the bathroom with the door closed, I would like you to knock and ask if it would be okay to come in before you open the door."
10. "I'd like you to prepare supper more often." Is this specific? How would you make it more specific?

PART THREE
_____

REAL LIFE ISSUES THAT
CONFRONT EVERY RELATIONSHIP

13

The Importance of Not Taking Things Personally

As children, we take what people say and what happens within our environment very personally. Our sense of attachment and security depends on our reading of what is going on around us.

So often our interpretations of what is going on around us are not an accurate depiction of the situation with which we are trying to cope. As children, our immature cognitive and emotional development does the best it can to make sense out of what is going on around us.

When mommy is angry or daddy is distant, we attempt to make sense out of what is taking place. To cope, we create storylines to make sense out of our experience. We come to identify who we are in terms of our storylines. As we have discussed before, our "inner critic" is a manifestation of these storyline conclusions that we arrive at as we go through life.

There is an ongoing negative cast to what the inner critic tells us. "I'm not good enough" or "I should be other than I am" are common themes that all of us encounter some time in our lives. I know someone who was told that if only they would change and "fit in" the family would be a happy place. The storyline associated with this was that "I am responsible for our family's problems." The inner critic put its stamp on this person by saying, "you are the cause of other people's upset."

To the extent that this goes on within us and to the extent that we are unaware of these dynamics, and clueless about their origin, we are at the mercy of our unconsciousness and lack of awareness

COMPASSIONATE COMMITMENT

about such things. To a certain extent, we are all stuck in the past, anticipating that the future will be a replay of what we have already experienced.

All of us have this process going on within us. We all carry our baggage around within us and we bring our various sensitive nerve-endings into every relationship we experience. If someone invariably touches one of our sensitive issues, we will react.

All too often, we see what our partner has said or done and we attribute to *them* the cause for our reaction and upset. As difficult as it may be, at first, to separate our partner from our reactions, to do so is the first step in correcting this pattern within ourselves. All our partner is doing is unknowingly setting us off in some way.

To be sure, once they realize that their words are serving as a trigger for our reactions, they need to be mindful of what they are saying to us. That is something that *they* have control over. Our being triggered and our reaction are ours to own and to deal with.

If you say something to me and I react to what you have said, that is my issue. If you become aware that by your saying something to me causes me to be upset, that becomes your issue. In both instances, we both need to become aware of what is taking place between us.

It is also essential that we realize that, apart from medical and hormonal issues, it is *our thoughts* that cause us to feel the way we do at any particular time. What we think determines how we feel. For example, you are in a lane of traffic that is forced to merge to the right to get to the tollbooth to pay your toll. You dutifully follow the directions to merge to the right and are slowly moving towards the tollbooth.

Then, you see a red sports car, in the lane that is being closed, moving up to the front of the line and merging in just ahead of the tollbooth. What kind of thoughts do you have about this driver's behaviour? How do you feel about this behaviour on the part of the person who cuts into line? In our Couples Classes at Kaiser, the class members universally felt resentment and anger.

Then, you find out that the driver had just received a cell phone call telling him that his five-year-old daughter had been hit by a bus and was being taken to the emergency hospital, and that her condition was serious. How do you feel about his cutting into line now? Our class members uniformly showed compassion and said that they would have, without hesitation, pulled to the side of the road to let him pass. *Again, our thoughts determine how we feel.*

Practical Applications of Not Taking Things Personally

Instead of falling into the trap of taking things personally, in our commitment relationship we need to affirm that we are a team, and as a team we form a partnership to work together to address whatever concerns we might have. We are, in our best moments allies and not adversaries.

So, How Best to Keep Our Focus Where It Belongs?

We would be well served to focus on the actual problem. We need to be in the present, in the now of life, not rehashing the past or in rehearsing for the future. Is the problem not having enough money? Is the problem not having enough time or energy for intimacy? Is it that our work schedule interferes with family time? Is the problem that one of our mothers is ill and needs our assistance, and by providing that assistance, we have less time available for one another? Or, is the problem that there are more demands on our time during the day than we can keep up with?

With such factors in our lives, we can easily begin to simply drift off in our own world of frustration and isolate ourselves from our teammate. The need is to realize that no single team member can take responsibility for how the team attempts to relate to those demands that involve both of you.

The need is to identify the exact nature of the problem that you're facing. If it is your financial situation, have you ever looked at what could be adversely affecting it?

- Is the amount you're spending on eating out more than you can afford on your budget?
- Do you even have a budget that takes into account all of the financial demands that you face in a given month?
- What about rent or mortgage payments and insurance expenses?
- What about child care demands, the costs, the logistics of getting our children where they need to be, when they need to be there?

It really helps to actually see how much your utility bill costs, how much your communication devices cost, how much your gas bill for the car is each month, or what your commuter costs or your grocery bill are on a monthly basis.

There is a huge benefit to having a couple's business meeting on a weekly basis, where the two of you deliberately set time aside to review what the week holds for you financially and logistically.

Stress is created by the belief that you have inadequate resources to cope with the demands that we face. The more isolated we feel in being confronted with the challenges with which we feel inadequate to cope, the more stress we experience.

What is the solution to such stress?

1. Realize that you are a team member and need to work together to relate with problems that impact both of you.
2. Specifically identify a problem.
3. Set up a plan that facilitates addressing the specific problem or problems that are causing you upset.

The weekly couple's business meeting allows you to sit down together and review what is possibly going to happen during the week, along with making plans, actually setting up a schedule to address what needs to get done:

- Who is going to go to which store to shop for what?
- Who is going to pay what bills?
- How much are you going to pay on your various bills?
- Who is going to take the kids to childcare?
- Who is going to pick up the children from childcare?
- Who is going to make the appointment for the doctor's visit?
- Who is going to make the breakfast or pack the lunches or be responsible for the dinner preparation?
- If you're going to get take-out for dinner, who is going to order, pay for and pick up the order? Out of which account is the money for the dinner coming?
- Who is going to do the dishes and clean up the kitchen?
- Who is going to be responsible for doing the laundry?
- When do you think you will want to be intimate?

In this way, you will not be caught by something that has not been factored into your attempts to take care of business. You will not find yourself faced with the need to pick up a child at daycare that you forgot about, or the sudden need to finish shopping for tonight's dinner. Such unexpected or unplanned for demands can send shockwaves through your nervous system and make life much more stressful.

Stress and fatigue are two of the forces that will often interfere with a couple's interest in sharing sexual intimacy. If you don't see yourselves as allies who are working together as a team, but instead feel like adversaries at odds with one another, being close and intimate can be the farthest thing from your mind. When you're working together and feel a sense of shared effort, often sharing intimacy will happen, and it will serve as a means of deepening the partnership that both feel as a result of working together.

14

Understanding More About Stress in Our Life

There's often confusion about the differences between stress and anxiety in our lives. Stress is our body's reaction to something that we're afraid of experiencing in the present. Anxiety is the anticipation of facing something that we are afraid of in the future. Our body's response to both stress and anxiety is similar.

Common themes of stress in our lives include:

- Being in one place feeling that you need to be someplace else.
- Never having enough time and energy to do what needs to be done.
- Feeling that you don't have the capacity to do what needs to be done.
- Feeling a sense of responsibility for being in control of things in your environment and if you're not in control, things will get out of hand and even become dangerous.

Essential Ways to Reduce the Stress Factor in Our Lives

There are two kinds of stress. There is the kind that we feel before we're going to give a speech or ask someone to marry us, or asking for a pay raise, or having been given a promotion to a more demanding position. Then, there is the kind of stress that comes from encountering something that we are afraid of facing in the present moment.

The first kind of stress is called "eustress" and we experience this when exciting positive things are happening in our lives and we feel a natural sense of positive excitement. This is often referred to as "good" stress. The more we experience this kind of stress, the *better* we are able to handle it in our lives without having the kind of reactions that survival stress requires of us.

The second kind of stress has been a developmental part of our survival system over the millions of years that we have evolved as a species. In the past, it has served us well as a survival supporter. When we would hear a twig break, we took exceptional care to see whether a sabre-toothed tiger was stalking us for an easy meal, or whether or not it was the wind that caused a twig to make a sound.

This survival stress mobilizes our fight, flight or freeze mode when encountering a potential threat. It lasts as long as the potential threat is present and subsides when it goes away. At such times of potential threat, our heart rate increases significantly, as does our blood pressure. Our breathing becomes rapid and shallow, muscles tense, and the body braces for action. Our digestive system both tenses and slows down, often causing nausea or stomach butterflies. Our surface blood vessels contract creating cold hands and feet, and pale skin colour. In such circumstances, this is a positive, helpful response because it prepares the threatened person for action when there's an immediate danger. With fear our focus is outside of ourselves. We're dealing with the *now* of our experience.

For anyone who has experienced the dreaded "anxiety attack," the description of these bodily responses will sound familiar. An anxiety attack is actually our bringing of our awareness to the way our body prepares itself to protect us when we *anticipate* facing something we are afraid of in the future. It is our fearful anticipation of facing something that magnifies our awareness of our body's response process so that our bodily response becomes incorporated into a part of our fear response.

COMPASSIONATE COMMITMENT

So often, the act of experiencing an anxiety attack causes fear that the attack itself will harm us. Often there is a fear that "I might die, I might have a heart attack, I can't breathe, I'm going to have a stroke."

As difficult as it might be to do, just remember that the symptoms you're experiencing in an anxiety attack are intended to make sure that you survive your threatening experience. And, as we have said before, it's our fearful anticipation of facing something that magnifies our awareness of our body's response process. To have a survival mechanism that results in your dying would be totally counter-productive.

In the modern day, our bodies often have this same intense physical response to fear or stressful situations, even when we don't need to "gear up" or run away. It's the triggering of this response when we don't need it that causes the problem of irrational thoughts including fear, anxiety, depression and fear-based conflicts between partners who are committed to one another.

Our body is a marvellous instrument. After it has mobilized itself to survive, there's a balancing process that's intended to restore it to its normal level of functioning. If our thinking continues along the lines of what has triggered the anxiety in the first place, we stay stuck and we continue to feel frightened. A sustained period of being stuck in fear is not healthy for our bodies.

The important thing to keep in focus is that what is triggering the anxiety is the anticipation of facing something in the future that you are *afraid* of experiencing. Certain thoughts will set this reaction process off. Even an untrue thought that we hold onto can serve as the trigger for our anxiety reaction. "*Suffering occurs when we believe in a thought that is at odds with what is true, what was true and what will be true.*"—Adyashanti

More on Relating to Stress in the Moment

When we have a stress reaction to some thought or situation that is causing us to suffer, we need to "stop, look and listen." We need to stop our simply reacting, look at what is going on with our behaviour and listen to what we are thinking. The more caught up we are with our reactions, the less we are able to relate to what is going on within us.

We need to get out of our reactive free fall and ground ourselves in the now. That means that we feel the pressure of the ground against the bottoms of our feet. If we are sitting, we need to feel the pressure of the seat against our bottoms and the small of our back. We need to take the frightening trigger thought and hold it against the reality of what is true, in the present moment.

The sense that a child has of being powerless, at the mercy of others or a situation, lasts until adulthood, unless it is addressed in a way that allows things to be seen from the perspective of an adult reality. Unless that adult reality is experienced, we will continue to behave and react as would a four-year-old who was scared out of his or her skin.

So, how do we accomplish this transformation from being a terror-stricken child to being an adult? We go from rehashing the past experience, to being in the present moment. Part of that transition is the emotional realization that I am no longer a child at the mercy of others who are able to control my life and force me to do what they want me to do. *I am an adult who has the power to say NO!* I am no longer at the mercy of my reactive thinking. I have a way of mindfully looking at what is going on within me that allows me to break my reactive cycle. This is true for dealing with anxiety. It is also true for dealing with any emotional response that our thoughts trigger within us. *"Stress is an alarm clock that lets you know you've attached to something not true for you."*—Byron Katie

Programs, like the Mindfulness Based Stress Reduction Program that was created by Jon Kabat-Zinn at the University of

COMPASSIONATE COMMITMENT

Massachusetts and the Kaiser Behavioral Education classes, deal with behavioral life issues that are based on *mindfully* responding to anxiety, stress, anger, depression and couples communication. The one constant in approaching life mindfully is that we need to be in the *present moment*. Being in the present moment is the key to restoring our equilibrium when we are under stress or feeling anxiety, anger or conflict between our self and others. In the following chapter we will discuss what Mindfulness is and specifically how it works in dealing with stress, anxiety, depression and anger.

15

Exactly What Is Being Mindful All About?

Mindfulness is the practice of bringing our awareness into the present moment, without judgment and with compassion. Mindfulness originates from the teachings of the Buddha 2,600 years ago.

What Is Awareness?

Adyashanti writes: "Awareness is that part of us that perceives, observes and witness our thoughts, feelings, behaviours, and body. It can be quite transformative to realize that you are not what you thought you were, that you are not your feelings, that you are not your beliefs, that you are not your personality, that you are not your ego. You are something other than that, something that resides on the inside, at the innermost core of your being. For the moment we are calling that something awareness itself."

Eckhart Tolle writes, "I am not my thoughts, emotions, sense perception and experiences. I am not the content of my life. I am life. I am the space in which all things happen. I am consciousness. I am the Now. I Am."

When our awareness is in the present moment, we are in touch with who we really are, with our very essence.

What Is in the Present, in the Now?

Being in the present is being one with each heartbeat and each in-breath and each out-breath, from moment to moment. We only have our next breath, our next heartbeat. Jon Kabat-Zinn wrote: "The past and future are only concepts, we only have the now…"

What Is It That Prevents Us from Being in the Present Moment?

Our reactive thinking prevents us from being in the present moment. From our earliest life encounters, our reactive thoughts create storylines about our experiences.

We bring our cognitive and emotional development as a young person to our experiences of parents, family, love, safety and fear.

In our storylines, we come to conclusions about ourselves and our world and make judgments about who we are, about whether or not our needs and feelings are ok or not. Our *inner critic* is a creation of these storyline-based conclusions we reach about who we are.

It is essential that we realize that we are not our thoughts. We are not our storylines. We are not who our inner critic says we are.

When we are being run by our reactive thinking, we are filled with fear, ignorance, judgments, myths, interpretations about ourselves and others and storylines. We are incomplete, never good enough, always striving for completion.

The Difference in Our Thinking When We Are or Are Not in the Present…

When our awareness is in the present, we are no longer scattered, we are at one with ourselves in the moment. We are at home with our *inner essence*. Who we are is the witnessing, observing awareness of our thoughts and feelings, our doubts, our fears and suffering. When we are in the present moment, we are able to *watch* our thoughts and feelings as we would watch water flowing over a waterfall.

Eckhart Tolle writes: "When you completely accept this moment, when you no longer argue with what is, the compulsion to think lessens and is replaced by an alert stillness. You are fully conscious, yet the mind is not labeling this moment in any way. This state of inner non-resistance opens you to the unconditional consciousness that is infinitely greater than the human mind. This vast intelligence can then express itself through you and assist you, both from within and from without. That is why, by letting go of inner resistance, you often find circumstances change for the better."

By contrast, when we are caught up in our storylines, we are *listening* to our words and become hooked by the storyline and either reliving the past or rehearsing for what we anticipate we will experience in the future based on what we have experienced in the past.

When we are in touch with our awareness, our thoughts reflect an insight, creativity and wisdom far beyond anything that our reactive thinking can imagine. We move from a life of doing to find our identity, to a life of being who we are in the present moment.

"Mindfulness meditation is an opportunity to reintroduce yourself to you… meditation is an act of loving yourself."—Jon Kabat-Zinn

We Are Awareness and We Are a Source of Compassion

What is special about each one of us is that, in addition to our being the awareness that is able to witness our thoughts and reactions, we are also a source of compassion. His Holiness The Dalai Lama wrote the following about compassion in *The Essence of the Heart Sutra*:

"According to Buddhism, compassion is an aspiration, a state of mine, wanting others to be free from suffering. It's not passive

COMPASSIONATE COMMITMENT

– it's not empathy alone – but rather an empathetic altruism that actively strives to free others from suffering. Genuine compassion must have both wisdom and lovingkindness. That is to say, one must understand the nature of suffering from which we wish to free others (this is wisdom), and one must experience deep intimacy and empathy with other sentient beings (this is lovingkindness)."

Jon Kabat Zinn has written that "When we are truly present, in the now, our natural state of being is to be compassionate, to feel empathy with another person or living being."

Typically, we are critical about ourselves, our thoughts, our actions, our abilities, our bodies and the list goes on and on. By continuing to be critical of ourselves, by judging ourselves as not being ok, we are doomed to relive our suffering. Instead of bringing judgment to what we have been thinking and feeling, we have the capacity to bring compassion, this ability to feel empathy for our suffering along with the wish to act on these feelings to alleviate the suffering.

According to Tara Brach, "Our suffering becomes a gateway to the compassion that frees our heart. When we become the holder of our own sorrows, our old roles as judge, adversary or victim are no longer being fueled. In their place, we find not a new role, but a courageous openness and a capacity for genuine tenderness, not only for ourselves but others, as well. Our capacity for compassion is the antidote to our negative judgments and our suffering.

"We have within us the capacity to hold our suffering as a mother would hold an uncomfortable, distressed infant. For us to be able to acknowledge what is going on within us, to allow for what we are going through, without judgment, for our suffering to be held in an embrace of loving-kindness and compassion "*frees our heart.*" In this we are able to move on and to begin to heal from the suffering that has kept us stuck in living with fear, anxiety, shame, guilt, anger and with a sense of not being good enough."

On another level, by being present with ourselves, we are also less reactive in relation to those with whom we come into contact. By reducing the conflict within ourselves, we are able to reduce the conflict between others and ourselves. Outer peace in the world begins with our achieving peace within us.

16

Seeing Anger for What It Is

Anger, for many, is a frightening emotion. As a child, experiencing anger in relation to adults can make us feel vulnerable and helpless. Such experiences can make *our* feeling anger uncomfortable. It can also make our experiencing anger in relation to our partner uncomfortable.

Anger is like a blinking red light on our dashboard. *"It is not the anger that needs to come out, but the pain that underlies the anger,"* writes Matthew McKay, Peter D. Rogers and Judith McKay in *When Anger Hurts*.

Exactly what **is** anger? Anger is our response to hurt. Underlying our hurt is an unmet need. When we find ourselves feeling anger, we need to ask ourselves "what am I hurting about? What unmet need am I experiencing, in this present moment?" When we are able to identify what it is that our unmet need is, our anger *dissolves*. It is that simple, really.

What follows from this inquiry requires facing issues and experiences that have caused us pain. From this simple inquiry follows some intensely felt feelings about others and ourselves in our life.

Anger serves the purpose of protecting us from and is, often, a substitute for feelings of:

- guilt
- loss
- anxiety
- fear
- emptiness

- embarrassment and shame
- hurt
- feeling trapped or helpless
- being bad, wrong or unworthy
- frustration of desire
- insignificance

Our being angry serves as a protective layer that allows us to avoid feeling painful feelings. Our anger gives us the illusion of being powerful. It allows us to forget the other person's needs. It gives the conviction of rightness. The more we allow our anger to serve as a buffer for our actually experiencing our feelings, the longer we put off facing and dealing with our hurtful feelings and the underlying unmet needs that our feelings are symptomatic of in our lives.

Instead of allowing our anger to be a barrier that prevents us from dealing with our pain:

- we need to deal with the source of our fear
- recognize our inner critic that leaves us feeling badly or worthless
- examine what makes us feel guilty
- face loss in our life
- saying what hurts or what bothers us
- problem-solve issues that need to be addressed
- connecting with others who can be a source of support

So often when we need to be close with someone who cares for us, our anger serves as a wedge that drives the very person we want to be close with away from us. Our anger leaves us empty and always with a tinge of guilt for how we have behaved or for what we have said.

As we have shared before, what we feel is not the fault of our partner. What we feel is the result of *our thoughts* only. According to Byron Katie, "No one has ever been angry at another human being. We're only angry at our story of them. The world is my perception of it. I see only through the filter of my story."

It is important to know that there is an *anger cycle* that we can become caught up in and by which we are controlled, until we are able to become conscious of what is actually happening within our emotional world. Once we become aware of what our pain is about, our anger evaporates.

The anger-cycle begins with our being under some kind of stress. Either we are tired or are frustrated by something. These stressors can serve as the frustrated energy that makes us susceptible to certain *triggering thoughts* that need to be thought before we actually become angry.

According to McKay, Rogers and McKay, there are two categories of trigger thoughts: The first has to do with our having *a sense of being entitled* about something. The second has to do with belief that *others are responsible for how we are feeling, others are responsible for our pain.*

The first category of trigger thoughts that are needed to feel anger is based on things that we feel should happen in relation to our lives.

The entitlement fallacy – My anger is because I deserve or want something that I don't have.

The fallacy of fairness – You are not being fair.

The fallacy of change – "I can control your behaviour."

The fallacy of conditional assumptions – "If you really loved me, you would do what I want."

The letting it out fallacy – "People who hurt me should be punished."

I am always struck by how these trigger thoughts sound so much like what a young child would say: "I want," "you're not being fair," "if you really loved me," or the fantasy that a child might have that they can control other people's behaviours.

The second category of trigger thoughts has to do with blaming other people for our pain.

Good-bad dichotomizing – "Something is always right/wrong, good/bad."

Assumed intent – "You meant to hurt me."

Magnifying – "You're *always* too busy," "you *never* listen to what I have to say," "*every* time I ask for something, you say no."

Global labeling – "You're always rationalizing things," "you're an idiot," "you only care about yourself."

The isolation that our painful experiences have caused us to feel and the loneliness that our unmet needs carries with them can easily lead us to cutting ourselves off from those with whom we most need to be close. Instead of closing ourselves off from our loved one, we need to affirm that it is our thoughts that cause us to feel the way that we do, and the fact is that ours is a partnership, my partner is my ally, not my adversary.

What Causes You to Get Angry?

Our task is to see what storylines we have created in our effort to make sense out of our experiences that have caused us pain and suffering. The following questions might assist in understanding what is causing us to feel anger, pain and unmet needs.

Matthew McKay, Peter Rogers and Judith McKay also suggests that we attempt to identify any unmet need that accounts for this pain, specifically from our past or in relation to our partner, in the present moment. We need to ask ourselves the following questions:

- If you didn't get angry, what feelings would you have to face?

COMPASSIONATE COMMITMENT

- How is your anger protecting you from your feelings?
- How did members of your family express their anger?
- How did you learn to express your anger the way you do?

There are several universal "Do's" and "Don'ts" that are helpful to keep in mind when you have a conflict with your partner, or anyone else.

- Stay away from making your differences into a right or wrong, win or lose situation.
- Deal with issues as they come up rather than gathering a long list of things that have caused you upset.
- Practice *kind speech* when relating with your partner, especially when dealing with issues that have caused pain and suffering between the two of you. *Kind speech* is a concept in Buddhist Psychology that advocates speech that is *honest, helpful, timely and kind.* If what you have to say is not honest, helpful, timely and kind, then silence is an act of kindness.
- One practice in dealing with differences with someone that is often effective is to *reverse* your position in relation to what is going on between you and your partner. If you are totally against a position, simply allow yourself to take the opposite position that you are so adamantly opposed to. Remember, it is our thoughts that impact how we feel about something. Our reversing our position allows us to have different thoughts about what is being discussed and through this reversal of our position, we might clear the way to be open to what we had been opposing.
- If things do not seem to be getting better, in a dialogue between yourself and your partner, take a *"time out."* A time out allows both of you to take a step back from what is going on between you.

A "time out" is an agreement between the two of you that says, when one of you feels the need to take a break from your interaction with one another that is ok. All you have to do is to express your need to step away for the time being. There are several ground rules that go along with taking a "time out." The agreement is that you will stop talking with one another for a period of one hour.

- You will disengage from what you are talking about and do something that allows your head to clear, take a walk, exercise, meditate.
- You are not to talk about what is going on between you and your partner with someone else.
- You agree to touch bases in one hour.
- If more time is needed to clear your head, you will renegotiate your reconnecting between the two of you.
- Your commitment is to reconnect and continue to address whatever issue you are addressing. No one is running away or abandoning the field and leaving their partner in an unfinished, frustrated place.

Differences between couples are a common occurrence. How we address our differences is what matters. Realizing that *we* are responsible for our feelings and that *our* feelings have a basis in our feeling pain and that *our* pain is the result of our having unmet needs, are important understandings we need in order to make resolving our differences possible.

It is also important to view our partner as someone who cares for us and wants us to feel loved and cared for. Our days of feeling as if we are alone, isolated and at the mercy of others, belong in our past, not in our present. Our storylines no longer have to control our lives. We can be in the present, with each breath and in each moment. We can share ourselves with the person that we love and are committed to in a full and genuine way.

*A profound note of appreciation is felt in being introduced to the work of Matthew McKay and his co-authors, whose book *When Anger Hurts*, was used as the text for our Kaiser Anger Management Courses.

17

Sexual Sharing: The Many Faces of Intimacy

Our sexual development corresponds with our personal, emotional development in life. We travel through seasons of exploration and experimentation as teenagers and young adults. Our experiences of how our needs and feelings were viewed and either respected or disregarded, laid the foundation for how comfortable we are with physically and emotionally undressing ourselves and being naked in front of someone else. How we were treated by significant others in our formative years also helped to determine how we view other people and how we regard their needs and feelings, their comfort and discomfort around sharing in moments of intimacy.

Sexual sharing with another is a process through which we come to understand each partner's comfort levels about being intimate and physical with one another. It is a matter of becoming aware of what you are comfortable in expressing with one another. The best practice is to travel at the rate of speed, in what is shared between the two of you, of the *least comfortable* partner. To try to force someone to do something that they are uncomfortable doing is not a caring way to relate to someone we profess to love. Carried to its most extreme, forcing oneself onto one's loved one who is not comfortable with what is being asked of them, is a hostile act and a form of spousal rape. Only hurt and resentment will follow from such an experience. What is sexually ok is to be determined by the two partners, together.

Sexual sharing is more than just the act of foreplay and intercourse. It is an atmosphere, the creation of an environment between two partners. It involves listening and being present with one another. It involves treating one another as the important person you are to each other. It involves caring behaviours and supportive and thoughtful encounters throughout the days and weeks of a lifetime.

This is not intended to suggest that the shared act of being sexually active with one another doesn't involve sensual kissing, caressing and exploring one another's bodies, heavy breathing and passionate, intense sexual activity. Our sexual life together is the whole package of all of the above.

An aspect of allowing yourself to open up emotionally with someone who is trustworthy, to allow yourself to become vulnerable with someone who you trust loves you, is to be put in touch with the unresolved pain that, on some level, we all carry around within ourselves. One couple shared with me that after having been intimate with one another, one partner began sobbing and wanted to be held tightly. The other partner was perplexed and concerned about what was taking place. The woman shared what she had gotten in touch with as a result of having opened herself up with the man who she had come to trust with her emotional life.

Her pain was something that had been a part of her since she was a young girl. She had always wanted to feel safe with her feelings with those adults who were supposed to be to be trustworthy in her life. Her mother's boyfriend sexually molested this woman as an eleven-year old. It wasn't until she was with this loving, trusted partner, with whom she felt safe in connecting with her feelings that these feelings and this experience was able to come to the surface.

One of the gifts of being a loving, trustworthy partner is that your being the person you are, allows your partner to get in touch with deeply felt painful issues. These issues often result in feelings of anger that have never before been able to come to the surface. It is important to see what is going on for what it is and to realize that when your partner begins to express their hurt and anger, you are not being wrongfully dumped on by someone who is being abusive in their treatment of you.

Your compassion and trustworthiness has allowed your partner to safely enter into the dark areas of their inner world. When this season of discovery is entered upon, intense feelings come to the surface and it is often helpful to see someone who is trained to relate to such issues. Such a trained counselor can assist your partner in making sense of what they are emotionally experiencing. Your role in this season of emotional discovery is to be supportive of your partner in their discovery process and for you to relate to whatever issues, *within yourself,* that are being triggered by the interaction that is taking place between you and your partner. A trained counselor can be of immense help for the two of you during these times of inner discovery.

Some Reflections on Affairs

For a woman or a man who is married to be blinded to any and all other men and women in their lifetime, is not only unreal, it is also not possible. We are, over the course of our lifetimes, going to meet many lovely, physically attractive, emotionally compelling people who we will find to be attractive. In addition, if you experienced your partner as being pretty, handsome, sexy, cute and desirable, isn't it possible someone else might also appreciate the person with whom you have chosen to share your life? What we do about these experiences is what makes the difference.

A golden rule about our being attracted to someone other than your partner, is *to respect the attraction.* Use it as an opening, an opportunity, to look inside to see what is going on within your emotional world to see what emotional issue or unmet need you have, that is not being addressed or met?

We are always going to have unmet needs. It is what we do with them not that we have them, that matters. This is especially true during the strained times that all couples have in their relationships.

When we find ourselves attracted to someone other than our partner, it can be viewed as a gift. It is an opening to look inside to see what it is that we are getting in touch with, what unmet needs are coming to the surface, what hurt and resentment we are feeling in the moment.

After we have done some personal inquiry about what is taking place inside of us, we can share our discovery of what we feel is going on within us, with our partner. This allows for the acknowledgment of your experience to be shared and for the two of you to address what it is that you are experiencing. Any attraction you might have is only a symptom of what is going on inside of you. In following this path, you are honouring your need, you are honouring your relationship with someone who cares about you and you are mindfully addressing any issue that needs to be addressed.

Tara Brach has written in her book, *True Refuge*, about this process of acknowledging our needs, rather than acting them out. She talks about the anachronism R.A.I.N:

R is for "recognizing our thoughts, emotions, feelings or sensations that are effecting us. It is recognizing that we are reacting to something and to recognize whatever is taking place as simply being there."

A is for allowing what is taking place within us to be what it is. "We do not attempt to fix or avoid anything. If we experience judgments about ourselves, allowing for them to exist does not mean that we agree with them. Rather, we honestly acknowledge our judgments and any painful feelings and unmet needs that exist within us."

I is for investigating what our feeling relates to within our life. It is not an invitation to become cerebral; it is an opportunity to connect the dots in terms of what is going on that is making us experience what we are experiencing. Tara Brach describes this as "asking yourself what most wants attention? How am I reacting to my body? What am I believing? What does this vulnerable place want from me? What does it most need?"

N is for nurturing, holding in our emotional arms the unmet need we are carrying around within us, as a mother would care for an upset infant. "Self-compassion naturally begins when we recognize that we are suffering."

N in some versions of R.A.I.N. also stands for our not being identified with our suffering. If we are not our thoughts and it is our thoughts that determine how we feel, by not identifying with our thoughts, we free ourselves from any limited sense of who we are.

A final note on acting out our needs and in following our impulse to pursue extramarital involvements: Such a course would be hurtful to our partner.

A strong sense of guilt is always a side effect of such a course. This is a path that will involve lying and cheating and, for many, it isn't what we are going to be comfortable with as a way of living life. It is far better to treat any such attraction as an opening to see what is asking to be addressed within us, rather than to act out our perceived need. In following a course of such internal inquiry, we will only become more aware of ourselves and more insightful as a committed partner.

Conscious Endings

With some couples, at some point, there may be an impulse to end a relationship. This sort of thinking reflects frustration and a realization that something is not as we would want it to be in our lives. Often such frustration is the result of not having effectively addressed an issue of concern. This is evident in those relationships where co-existing has taken place. Often such impulses to abandon the relationship take place around life transitions, the "empty nest" or retirement or realizing that our life is in its winter season and we still have things in our "bucket list." This is an example how kicking a can down the road results in running out of road.

Another season that can come upon us as a relational partner, that can beckon us to consider leaving a commitment relationship, is when, in our travelling through life together, our partner decides to sit down by the roadside and not be interested in travelling on together. Carl Jung, the noted Swiss psychoanalyst has written, at such a time the one who still is involved in exploring and expressing themselves in new ways can choose to sit down beside their partner and can remain with them, or they can decide that, to be true to who they are, they must continue walking down the road of life alone. Such a decision is not made lightly and involves pain and sadness and it is a course that some must take to remain authentic to who they are in their life process.

The truth of the matter is that it takes as much work to consciously end a relationship as it does to work out a relationship. Consciously ending a relationship so that you can go on with your life, without carrying unfinished business into your future relationships, requires as much work as it does to consciously work on what needs to be addressed in your present relationship so that it can continue. Without a conscious ending to a present relationship, you are not free to be present with someone else.

18

The Adventures of Becoming a Parent

When a woman becomes pregnant, her whole emotional and hormonal world changes. Her focus becomes inward directed into the profound event that is taking place inside of her. Her partner will experience a change in this inward focus and may feel hurt that they, as a couple, are no longer the primary object of the-mother-to-be's attention. The man's role during this time of bringing a new life into the world is to become comfortable with being the *support* person for the woman whose body is undergoing a nine-month journey that is totally out of their control.

Any issues the prospective father has of feeling abandoned by their spouse during pregnancy and after the arrival of the new little person, needs to be addressed and resolved. Often a partner, typically a man, who has not received the kind of attachment to their mother that they needed as a child, will find a woman with whom they finally receive that connection. When the new baby comes along, several things need to be understood. First, the unmet needs of the past are *not* going to be met. The time for receiving this attachment with a maternal figure is in the past.

Second, if a father tries to maintain the couple's experiences that he had prior to the pregnancy it will be resented by the new mother. The new mother's role is to be the mother to this new life and not to her spouse. So, the impetus needs to be with *both* partners to acknowledge that the needs of the newborn are the priority for both parents. And, the husband with unmet attachment issues needs to mindfully address their underlying need for mothering.

It is important to appreciate that dealing with such issues is not an insurmountable process. What can be insurmountable is to not realize that this issue exists and to become caught up in a powerful need dynamic that, if left to fester, can truly injure the relationship between partners and with the child. This needn't happen. This is a common dynamic that, if mindfully addressed, will in time, become a non-issue.

Becoming New Parents

Whether or not the quality of care the new parents are providing for their new little person is ok, every couple that has their first baby feels at a loss about what to do and is feeling their way in the dark about being parents. Even experienced pediatric nurses who give parenting classes to new parents, begin at ground zero in their readiness for their new role as parent when they become the new mom or dad. It becomes a standing joke that when the teacher becomes the student, they must rely upon their fellow teachers to learn to change diapers, breastfeed and deal with other essential mothering tasks.

The reality is that new parents learn by trial and error. The key is to attempt to plug into what the infant's needs are, and that takes time. And just when you begin to feel like you are on the right path, a new wrinkle throws things into a state of uncertainty. This state of uncertainty is normal. All new parents experience this. It can become discouraging and annoying, and can reinforce a sense of helplessness. Whatever storylines you might have that suggest that you cannot do things properly will be certain to kick into high gear. The key is to not try to be a perfect parent. Why? Because there is no way a parent can be perfect.

Donald Winnicott, an English psychiatrist and pediatrician, has written it is the caring, attentive parents' imperfection, not meeting every need the child has, all of the time, that allows the child to grow into a healthy person who is able to deal with frustration in life. Instead of being "perfect," try to be "good enough." If you meet your child's needs seven out of every ten times, you're "good enough" and your child will thrive.

COMPASSIONATE COMMITMENT

*****

No matter how much both partners share in the baby's life, there is a division of labour that needs to be acknowledged and respected. In relationships where there is a biological mother and father, the mother is the primary caregiver for the infant and she will share that role with her partner. However, there are limits in what the partner can do in regard to nursing and in the primary establishment of attachment between infant and mother.

As much as the role of the father-to-be is one of support to the mother-to-be during pregnancy, that role of support system remains when the baby arrives. No matter how much sharing is done in responding to the needs of the new arrival, the woman is still emotionally and physically tied to the baby in a way that the father can't be.

The energy it takes for milk production, nursing and the transitioning of hormonal levels, the need for rest, the fact that the mother's maternal instincts has her emotionally always on alert regarding her new baby, is something that her partner will never quite be able to duplicate, no matter how caring the daddy might be.

The partner's role is to be supportive of the mother, to provide for respites for the mom. The father figure's job is to perform those tasks that keep the family team humming: shopping, doing the laundry, giving the mom some time-outs where she can be "off duty", to take a shower, to sleep longer, to read a book.

In one family I worked with, the wife had Sundays off for a good portion of the day. The husband-partner would take their little person out on Sunday morning and they visited nearly every playground in San Francisco. The son and dad enjoyed swings and slides and new sights and experiences together. The mom was able to shower and take a nap without being "on duty". This division of labour was essential to maintain an emotional and physical equilibrium for the long haul of transitioning from being a couple to being parents.

This is not to say that the father figure didn't share intimately in their son's daily life. He did. It was just that he had a fatherly role. He would change diapers and would rock and sing to the son in the rocking chair and play with him or read to him nightly. And, he was not the child's mother. The dad's role was to be a dad and to support the mommy so that she was able to have a full tank of gas to continue to meet the demands of motherhood. And, for him to be a fully loving, caring dad with his little one.

*****

Becoming a parent turns a searchlight onto every issue of our own childhood experiences that we need to revisit within ourselves. Our little one becomes the stimulus that brings us into contact with what it was like when we were "little ones" ourselves. We need to become conscious of those issues that are touched within us, so that we can be free to separate our experiences from our child's experience

It has been said that life is our teacher. An important part of our life is our partner and our children. To be open to what they put us in touch with as we travel our life's journey together is a gift for all.

19

Relating to Hormonal Changes That Are Out of Our Control

There are certain hormonal seasons that arise with our partner that are out of our and their control. A woman's period is one such example of a time when the woman is being influenced by hormonal changes that may impact her behaviour or what she says. Again, it is imperative that if your partner is being impacted by hormonal changes, to not take what she says or her behaviour personally. It is also imperative that what she is going through is not demeaned or ridiculed.

The same is true for when a woman becomes pregnant… her whole hormonal world is turned upside down. She has things going on within her for which she has totally no control. She is, essentially, on a nine-month journey where she is a passenger on a ride to which she can only submit, if she elects to move onto motherhood. Any semblance of having control is, for the most part, out of the picture. On the positive side of being pregnant, the mommy-to-be can feel the excitement of being in the process of bringing a new life into the world. The anticipation of parenthood is, for many, a time of joy and the offering of a sense of fulfilment.

After the delivery of a baby, the mother will also experience hormonal changes that correspond to where the body is in the adjustment period of new motherhood. Milk production requires certain levels of hormone adjustment within the new mother. These adjustments can stimulate mood changes. If sleep deprivation is added to this mix, often a new mom might feel physical discomfort and experience depression, as well.

Again, a woman will undergo hormonal changes during menopause. During this period of a woman's life, her body is transitioning from being able to procreate and no longer being able to become pregnant. The woman's whole hormonal world is undergoing a complete transition that impacts women differently, with varying degrees of intensity. There can be mood fluctuations, hot flashes and a sense of anxiety about being out of control of a woman's body and emotions.

Hormonal changes during these seasons in a woman's life need to be acknowledged and respected. A partner needs to be a supportive presence for the woman during these seasons. While it is important to be present and to listen to what your partner is saying during these periods of change, it is equally important to not personalize what they are saying.

I have heard women say that during their monthly cycle, or during their menopause, they can hear the words coming out of their mouths as they are saying something that they do not want to be saying. They also report they can't do anything about what is going on with them in that moment, and feel guilt for their behaviour and words.

Lonnie Barbach, a noted psychologist and a wonderful writer in the San Francisco Bay Area, wrote a book entitled *The Pause* that described her experiences of confusion, frustrations, doubts, mood swings, mix diagnosis from various physicians and sense of being in an unsettling place in life. It's a useful resource during this period in life.

*****

Hormonal changes are not the exclusive domain of women. Men go through hormonal changes as they become older. This change is referred to as andropause. It describes a drop in testosterone levels that many men experience as they age. A man's energy and ability to do what they used to do years before is not present. Such changes can impact how a man feels about himself.

COMPASSIONATE COMMITMENT

Such a season of change for a man is often highlighted by the man having difficulty with sexually performing as he ages. The frequency and intensity of lovemaking can be diminished and this can make a man feel as though he has lost something that had defined who he is. In addition, his strength, stamina and muscle mass lessen as he ages, which only reinforces that he is less of his masculine self than he used to be.

Such changes in a man need to be treated as lovingly as are the changes that a woman goes through as she progresses through the various seasons of life.

20

Living With Illness

Life is an arbitrary state of being. We are never sure about what will be from moment to moment. And, that is why for us to live in the present moment and not in the past or in the future makes so much sense. If we are living in the now and not reliving the past or anticipating the future, we are able to meet the present, in the present, free from the baggage of distorted thoughts and fears.

We are all bound to become ill at some point in our lives. We each have whatever DNA we are born with. Some have severe immune deficiency issues while others do not. Some have a propensity for allergies, others don't. Some have issues with hearing or sight. Some have strong bones. Some have illnesses that will end their lives in childhood, while others will live to be 100. I have always looked at others who are suffering, when I am not suffering, and say to myself, "there, but by the Grace of God, go I." Life, our physical health, is that arbitrary.

When we are committed to someone we love, and our lives are intertwined with someone else, we, again face a double dose of the arbitrary nature of life. The healthy partner who suffers a stroke at age 39, the young 35-year-old woman who develops breast cancer, the 26-year-old who is hit by a car and suffers paralysis from the waist down, the person who contracts AIDS, or who takes antibiotics that eliminates their necessary intestinal bacteria and is overtaken by bacteria that invades their body causing chronic illness. The fifty year old who begins to manifest symptoms of dementia.

And we, as partners who love and live with someone, are committed to caring for them through "sickness and health." We are faced with the possibility and responsibility of relating to all of these possibilities should they arise.

The more we are able to approach our care-taking role *as a team* with our partner, the better. So often a partner resists being in the role of the one who is in need of assistance. By working together, we can minimize the discomfort that our partner may have in being dependent on us.

What is true is that we can each become the one who needs to be cared for. The role of being the "contained," the one in need of support and the "container," the one who provides the support, goes back and forth between partners over the course of a relationship. Realizing that we can take turns being in need and providing assistance for our partner's needs is a part of life. The realization that as partners we are truly teammates can help to normalize our roles as the recipient or the provider of assistance in our relationship.

Being in the present moment is our natural state of being. It is the place where we can bring our awareness and compassion fully into whatever it is that requires our attention. We need to live in a reality absent of delusional thoughts and fears that distort our reality. As Jon Kabat-Zinn wrote, "The past and future are concepts, we only have the present moment."

Something that goes along with living in the present moment is to know when we, as care-givers, need support ourselves, both in the actual providing of physical care for our partner and in receiving support for our role as a primary care provider for our partner.

There will be a point in our lives where we may well need assistance with physically caring for our partner. Physically we won't be up to lifting or moving someone. We need to be able to acknowledge our limitations when they become apparent to us. We need to be able to listen to those who care for our well-being when they express their perceptions of whether or not we are in need of more support in providing for our loved one's physical care.

Support groups are just that, support groups—people on the same journey who get together and share their experiences, helping to put issues and feelings into perspective. This is another form of "it takes a village" at work. It is important for us to know that others are sharing similar experiences, to hear other's expression of feelings about what is going on in their lives in their role as care provider for their partner. Such sharing opens the door to outside resources that without such support, we would not know about.

21

Living With the End of Life and Death

Death is something we, as human beings all share, no matter where we live, what we do, how materially wealthy we might be or how materially impoverished we are. Death is something that we all will experience. If truly appreciated, this realization can actually bring us together as members of the human family. It may even free us up to treat others as we would want to be treated, and live with the realization "but for the grace of God, there go I" in life.

Many people are afraid to think about death and dying. Many of us practice a form of magical thinking… if I don't think about it, maybe it won't happen or if I don't think about it, the idea of dying and the fear that goes along with those thoughts will be put off until sometime in the future. How many of us continually kick the "death can" down the road? The wills that we don't make, the decisions about our being cremated or buried, where our remains are going to be placed, with whom are we going to share the "dreamless sleep," are, often, not readily addressed.

As much as we might want to put off thinking about the inevitable, by being involved with someone else in a commitment relationship, we are forced to face the reality of the *impermanence* of life. This is the reality that all life ends, at some point in time. All life travels from birth to death, in all species. The reality is that if we are born, we *will* die. Our journey through life has a beginning and it has an end. It is an important aspect of life to share with one another. It might even make it less scary than if we were to be alone.

The death of a loved one opens us up to the pain of not having their presence with us as they used to be. The person next to us in bed, the person across the breakfast table in the morning, the person we shared many moments of closeness and happiness with, and the person we had come to know in all of their ways and words. The sound of their voice, not hearing them in the next room... all of these realities are what we are facing when our loved one is no longer physically with us.

The profound void and pain that our partner's absence has created in our lives is part of our grieving process. It is important to realize that the reality of having shared our lives with someone we have loved transforms us. In our sharing, our partner has become a part of *who we are* and in that, they will always remain with us.

Our partner's absence also thrusts us into areas that, because of their presence in our life, are unfamiliar to us. Those things that were a part of what they took care of—the finances, the shopping, car and home maintenance, paying the bills, managing retirement investments, reaching for the sugar in the cupboard, folding the laundry, vacuuming—with their death, they are no longer here for us to do what they used to do. It is now left up to us to fill in the void that their absence has created.

There is a very real and practical grieving process that takes place with a loved one's passing. There are numerous aspects of grieving: shock and denial, anger, guilt, bargaining, depression and acceptance. We will briefly explore these various aspects of the grieving process that Elisabeth Kubler-Ross has described in her book, *Death and Dying*.

To begin with, the *shock* of the loss of someone, no matter how long they have been ill or how much you think you have prepared yourself for their passing, is something that has a poignancy all of its own. It has to do with finality of their not being present with us anymore. In this shock, as Elisabeth Kubler-Ross has written:

- We can go into a period of *denying* the reality of their passing.

COMPASSIONATE COMMITMENT

- We can become *angry* that they have died and actually chastise them for leaving us and forcing us to have to deal with life issues that they had taken care of in our relationship.
- We can feel *guilt* for being angry with them and for having all of those angry and resentful thoughts that we have thought.
- We can attempt to *bargain* with ourselves to see if we could of, should of or would of done things differently it would have changed the outcome.
- We can go into a sense of *sadness and depression* about their passing and experience loneliness, emptiness and a sense of feeling lost.
- We might actually achieve some semblance of *acceptance* about the reality of our partner having died and the transition that we find ourselves in, as a result of their passing. We can then begin the process again, and again, and again until it runs its course. There is no one way that we can follow the course of *our* grieving process. We could go from acceptance to anger, to guilt, and back to acceptance. We go through this process, in our way, as many times as we need to heal from the pain of loss.

In reality, our *grieving process* is our human *healing process* around the loss of someone specifically or around loss in a more general sense. It has its own course to travel, depending on the person who is undergoing the journey. It takes as long as it takes. There is no "should" about what you need to do. No one else can tell you what's true for you in your process. In this regard, it is profoundly helpful to belong to a bereavement group to share with others who are similarly dealing with the loss of a loved one.

The Kaiser Bereavement Group that I was privileged to facilitate from time to time, met weekly. It was a drop-in group where people could attend or not as they chose. It was free. Some people would attend for months, some would attend for years depending on their needs.

One issue that would present itself quite frequently would be the *"Who Am I"* question that we are left with after we are no longer with our partner. In some instances, we had couples who had married after high school graduation, were married for over fifty years and one partner had served as the other's caregiver for twelve years prior to their partner's death.

When the partner died, the person left behind could say that they were the husband or wife of someone and they *were* their partner's caregiver but who are they now? In this lonely, painful time, stumbling around trying to deal with all of the issues that present themselves to the surviving partner, to have to rediscover who they are after years of having who they are identified by their relationship with their deceased spouse is a daunting process. For those of us who are separated from our partner, our accepting and relating to this question is its own teacher.

*****

Mary Grace Orr, a Senior Faculty Member of the Spirit Rock Meditation Center in Woodland California, has said that Buddhist Psychology can be summarized into three notions.

- This is the way it is
- Let go
- No one deserves your friendship and loving-kindness more than you

"This is the way it is" means just that. It is 99 degrees outside. Obama was elected President. The cost of eggs has gone up two dollars for a dozen. I am an asthmatic. I have a faulty heart valve. Due to my prostate cancer having metastasized, I have to take hormone therapy. I am not the same person I was thirty years ago. The notion is to accept what is, to face what is and to relate to what is, in the present moment.

"Let go" means not fighting what is, what you want it to be or what you feel it should be. What is profoundly powerful about such acceptance is that there is a thought shift when we accept *what*

COMPASSIONATE COMMITMENT

is and let go. It frees us up in ways we would not have anticipated. We become free from needing things to be one way or in having to feel able to control the uncontrollable. The importance that we have attached to something or someone is no longer the controlling force in our approach to life.

"*No one deserves your friendship and loving-kindness more than you*" allows us to befriend ourselves, to love ourselves. For many, to befriend yourself is a new experience. And it changes the balance of feeling we are not ok and incomplete, to we *are* ok and we are complete. *And*, it's ok to give yourself a hug. Instead of a scowl, give yourself a smile.

By embracing these notions about life and ourselves, we can make any life experience less traumatic. We can experience life as more forgiving and an avenue for learning, for becoming more aware and connected with our essence… with who we really are as a person.

Being in the now…
Letting go of what isn't…
Give yourself a hug…

22

What Place Does Counseling Have in a Commitment Relationship?

When it feels like there is a need to gain some helpful perspective on something that is causing a couple upset, seeing a professionally trained and licensed therapist only makes sense. The therapist cannot tell you what you need to do. They can, however, assist you in finding your way through the forest of confusion that you and your partner may be having about some issue or issues that you both feel need to be addressed.

How do you go about finding a therapist? Often those who we know and trust have seen someone for counseling or know people who have been in counseling. Seeing someone who your friends have seen is often the beginning step that leads to developing a counseling relationship with a trained counselor. Your primary care physician or a doctor you feel comfortable with can also suggest someone you might initially meet with.

The question is often raised, why go to a counselor when you can go to a friend or friends for support? Having a network of real friends is a precious aspect of life. A real friend may or may not be able to focus on you and your partner's concerns without bringing their views of what should be done into the picture.

With a trained, licensed counselor, their focus is on your experience only, on what is going on with you. They are not "friends" in the sense that your friends are your friends. Their focus and responsibility is to you, your needs and feelings and what is in your best interest, regardless of anything else.

COMPASSIONATE COMMITMENT

There are some things to keep in mind when you select someone to open up with and to trust with your feelings and vulnerabilities. To begin with, you and your partner need to feel *comfortable* with the person with whom you are going to entrust your well-being and that of your relationship. If there is any hesitation about your or your partner wanting to work with someone, it is ok to interview someone else. And, it is ok to interview as many therapists as needed before you decide upon someone.

Secondly, if you have questions about any aspect of the person with whom you will be sharing your needs and feelings, it is perfectly ok to ask them the questions that you would like to have answered. It would be appropriate to ask questions such as:

- How long have you been in practice?
- What kind of issues do you specialize in addressing with couples?
- Have you been or are you in a commitment relationship?
- What is your orientation as a therapist?
- How much therapy have you yourself undergone?

These are all legitimate inquiries to make of someone with whom you are going to entrust yourself and your relationship. Or, you may begin meeting with someone and right away feel comfortable sharing with them and decide that this is the person with whom you would like to work. It can be as simple as that.

There are as many views of how to approach counseling as there are practitioners in the field. Some are more oriented by one theory over others. There are those who look upon what they do as "treating a patient" and attempting to "cure" them of their problem.

There are those who approach working with individuals and couples where they are in life and walking with them through their experiences and attempt to make sense out of what is taking place in their relationship. The focus on the part of the therapist is on being *present* with the couple in relation to their questions, needs and feelings. In this approach the notion is that if the therapist looks at the person through the *lens* of some theory, they are not fully being *with* that person. I view my job as facilitating a person's and couple's discovery process and not to interfere with it. True healing comes from being *present* with someone—where they are, as they are.

Can a therapist work with couples and be fair to each person's perception of what is going on in their relationship? The answer is yes. This is possible when it is explained that two people can experience the same situation and have diametrically opposite experiences of the same event. One person's experience is to be treated as being equally valid as the other. There is no right or wrong in someone's experience of an event or happening. The only exception to this is if there is any abusive behaviour indicated. Their experience is their experience. We begin from there, respecting each person's experience and attempt to understand the reason for their differences.

When couples use the same words but speak different languages, it is possible to help translate the different languages they are speaking by respecting both people's experiences.

As a couple works as a team with one another in dealing with life issues, so too a counselor becomes a part of that team and can, with the assistance of the two partners, work to deepen their awareness and ability to work together for the long haul as lifelong partners.

What happens if only one of the partners feels the need to seek out a counselor to gain clarity and understanding about issues of concern? That is perfectly fine. What often happens is that any uncertainty about going to a counselor on the part of the reluctant partner is often dispelled when they experience the positive internal shifts that they can feel with the partner who is meeting with a counselor. Very often, the reluctant partner will actively join into the process.

COMPASSIONATE COMMITMENT

It used to be that therapy would or could last for months and years. Each couple's situation is different and requires individualized decisions that are appropriate to the couple's needs and progress. Today there is a trend in counseling and therapy to allow for fewer sessions spread over time. The notion is that much can come about as a result of a single session and to allow for what has transpired in a session to be worked through before having another session. In this format, a couple can meet for several sessions and then agree to call in to set up another appointment when they feel ready for the next session.

Needless to say, such an approach has its critics. I have worked with people for years at a time as part of their growth process. What I have found to be true is that the primary healing force in the therapy experience is the therapist being fully present with the individual or couple. Part of being present with them is to allow for their readiness for a next session to be something agreed upon by the couple and counselor and not just by a routine rescheduling of another session.

23

Some Final Thoughts About Compassionate Commitment

I have found that lessons are learned over years of sharing life with someone:

- The first lesson is that your partner's needs are as important as your own. In partnership with someone, by respecting your partner's needs, you are showing true consideration and love for them. This is a variation on the theme of treating a loved one as you would like to be treated. It is seldom that you can go wrong approaching one another in this way.
- In areas of important decision-making about life-impacting issues, it is better to have both of you on the same page. How to spend money, job selections, deciding upon where to live, whether or not to start a family right now, are decisions that are ideally made together with true respect for one another's concerns. Ideally, the decision-making process requires both partners being in agreement about a course of action. If either of you are not in agreement, it's best if the decision is not made until you are in agreement or have come to a compromise. Such decisions require dialogue and may require seeking out a counselor to facilitate the decision-making process.
- In dealing with how to handle money, a couple might agree to divide up the bills and for each to cover certain monthly expenses. In some relationships, one partner might prefer to not be involved with money issues at all. In the final analysis, each couple is a team who needs to

work together to decide how to handle their financial matters.
- It often works to have a household fund that pays for the bills, and a grocery fund that pays for the groceries. It is often easier to keep those two accounts separate. It is also helpful for each partner to have an account where they can have access to daily spending money. Working out such agreements paves the way for there to be a clear understanding about financial agreements between the two of you.

In those relationships where both partners work and have an income source, it stands to reason that each partner would have *their* account that also becomes, a joint account. Then, the two people can decide what comes out of which account for whatever need arises during the course of the month.

- The idea of working together in areas that require both to participate in decision-making, has been an essential focus in this discussion of Compassionate Commitment. Financial decisions, life-changing decisions like relocating, and health issues fall into this category of sharing. It is also important for each partner to have time to themselves for activities that are a part of expressing who they are as individuals. Art, music, activities, hobbies, need to be respected and encouraged by both partners. As Khalil Gibran has written, "Let there be spaces in your togetherness."

We began this journey together by viewing our relationship as a garden that needs to be tended to in order for it to thrive. To do that, we need to acknowledge our partner on a daily basis. We need to emotionally connect with one another by saying "I love you," and through gestures that say "I am thinking about you" each day that we share life together.

We need to share with one another what is going on in our lives. We need to be *present* and to *listen* to what our partner is experiencing and feeling.

We need to reconnect with one another by doing things for them that we know they like like giving them a back rub or pouring a cup of coffee. By regularly expressing these simple gestures of thoughtfulness and kindness it reinforces a sense of connection between two people.

We need to have fun with one another, to break the demand cycle of life and do something that will bring a shared moment of enjoyment to one another. Shared moments of good times build affectional bonds that strengthen our lives with one another.

And finally, we need to live a life where we bring our awareness into the present moment, without judgment and with compassion. We need to pause, to get in touch with what is going on in that moment, how we are feeling, what we are thinking, what our bodily sensations are in the now of our life experience.

We need to let the R.A.I.N. fall upon our life as individuals and as life partners to make sure that our relational garden thrives in our journey through life.

www.ingramcontent.com/pod-product-compliance
Lightning Source LLC
Chambersburg PA
CBHW020911080526
44589CB00011B/550